# CALGARY BUILDS

# CALGARY BUILDS

## The Emergence
## of an
## Urban Landscape
## 1905-1914

# by Bryan P. Melnyk

Alberta Culture/Canadian Plains Research
Center
1985

Canadian Cataloguing in Publication Data

Melnyk, Bryan Peter.
    Calgary builds

Includes index.
Bibliography: p.
ISBN 0-88977-038-7

1. Architecture - Alberta - Calgary. 2. Calgary
(Alta.) - Buildings. 3. Architecture and society -
Alberta - Calgary. I. Alberta. Alberta Culture.
II. University of Regina. Canadian Plains Research
Center. III. Title.
NA747.C34M44 1985    720′.97123′3    C85-091293-8

48,234

# Table of Contents

# Preface

There were fewer than three-quarters of a million people on the Canadian prairies in 1905, but by the time that World War I began, almost a million more were added. In the same period, Calgary's population multiplied more than sixfold, from approximately 12,500 to nearly 80,000. Along with this great torrent of immigrants came immense changes to the local economy, society and physical environment. In one short decade, Calgary was dramatically transformed from a small community on the frontier of an immature region into a progressive, fast-moving metropolis, the centre of a vast agricultural and natural resource hinterland. Rapid growth strained the capability of existing facilities to meet the needs of the expanding population. It soon became apparent that more substantial architecture was needed to keep pace with this development, and to create a new image for the city that was commensurate with its changed status.

This book is concerned with the more than ten thousand buildings that were erected between 1905 and 1914, particularly those that were constructed in response to favourable economic conditions during the boom years of 1909 to 1913. Using information from a variety of sources, including local newspapers, city records and directories, government publications, school board documents, architectural drawings, archival materials and secondary literature on western Canadian architectural history and on relevant topics pertaining to Calgary history, this study surveys the architectural landscape that emerged. It not only describes the architectural features of individual buildings, but also analyzes their importance within the broad context of the city's social, economic, cultural and technological development.

This research paper reveals that Calgary very quickly took on both the character and appearance of a modern North American metropolis in this period of unparalleled growth

1

and prosperity. It observes that the city entered into the mainstream of modern architectural design in conjunction with the sudden flourishing of the local economy. Skyscrapers, stores, apartment buildings and industries which utilized construction techniques devised in the United States sprang up in great numbers as opportunities for profit loomed large. Single-family residences also appeared in the thousands as workers immigrated to the city *en masse*. Yet while new architectural forms transfigured the urban landscape, this study shows that Calgary retained its distinctively British atmosphere in the midst of a fast-paced building boom. The palatial residences of the city's upper classes, elegant commercial structures and grand public buildings and schools manifested a certain preference for Edwardian architectural tastes. In the years leading up to the war, these edifices thus provided local residents with tangible evidence of their society's fundamental loyalty to British ideas and fashions, as well as their unswerving faith in the continued material progress of their community.

# Acknowledgements

The author gratefully records his obligation to all who assisted in one way or another in the production of this book. To the staff of the Glenbow-Alberta Institute Library and Archives, the Provincial Archives of Alberta, the Canadian Architectural Archives at The University of Calgary, the City of Calgary Planning Department library, and the library at Parks Canada, Western Regional Office, the author offers his sincere thanks. Thanks are also due to Dr. Henry Klassen, Dr. Robert Stamp, Dr. Janice Dicken-McGinnis, Dr. Hugh Dempsey, the History Department of The University of Calgary, and to Ms. Wynn Smith of the Calgary Public School Board and Jerry Fitzgerald of the Calgary Separate School Board. Special recognition should be given to Dr. Anthony Rasporich, also of The University of Calgary, for his patient scrutiny of early drafts of this work. Robert Hunter formerly of Alberta Culture, Historic Sites Service, is also thanked for his helpful comments.

# List of Tables

All photographs courtesy of Glenbow-Alberta Institute

4

# List of Illustrations

# Introduction

As Professor Robert Furneaux Jordan has lucidly observed, architecture is the product of a hundred circumstances.[1] Buildings are not merely physical structures erected to provide shelter and essential services for society. They are also art forms which reflect the skill of artisans and architects and which express the values, needs and wealth of the people for whom they are built. A study of historic buildings, therefore, can reveal much about the material and technological development, aesthetic tastes, cultural preferences, and socio-economic realities of a community. To the historian then, especially the urban specialist, architecture can be a rich and fascinating document of the past.

This book undertakes to examine the buildings that were erected in the city of Calgary between 1905 and 1914, particularly those built during the dynamic and prosperous boom period of 1909 to 1913. As well as describing the construction details, architectural features and stylistic derivations of a representative group of buildings, it will analyze these structures within the context of changes in the economy, population and social character of the city. A careful portrayal of Calgary's architectural landscape will provide some insight into the overall appearance of the city, as well as into the prevailing attitudes and level of affluence of the local citizenry. Before elaborating further on the approach of this study, however, it is necessary to take account of the literature on the general subject of western Canadian architecture.

To date, little scholarly attention has been devoted to the historic architecture of Calgary, or indeed of western Canada. This apparent dearth of interest may be attributed to the fact that the west is a young region relative to other parts of Canada and, as in other fields of endeavour, little information has yet been published. According to Harold Kalman, it is only since 1960 that mature treatments of Canadian architecture and specific works on older cities and provinces have begun to appear.[2] Furthermore, since no innovative design ideas or great works of architecture such as those associated with London, Paris and Chicago have originated in the west, architectural historians and critics have tended to ignore the region. It is not surprising, therefore, that western Canadian buildings have been categorized as unimpressive and thus unimportant.[3]

Nevertheless, in spite of the bias of earlier works, interest in the study of western Canadian architecture is on the upswing. Federal, provincial and municipal government agencies, concerned citizens, and professional and academic researchers have become increasingly involved in the subject. Much of this current fascination with architecture can be seen as the result of the incredibly rapid rate of development in many western centres, especially in Alberta, which has led in the recent past to the indiscriminate demolition of countless historic buildings. The loss of familiar landmarks, together with an increasing awareness of the virtues of preserving old structures, has in turn given rise to the establishment of several inventories which are aimed at compiling data on remaining buildings and, in some cases, delineating criteria for their conservation.[4]

Unfortunately, few publications on western Canadian buildings have emerged yet from these surveys, most of which are less than ten years old. Several reports, including Elaine Kendal's *The Development of Edmonton and Its Buildings to 1914*, Edward Mills's *The Early Court Houses of Alberta*, and R.R. Rostecki's *The Early Court Houses of Saskatchewan*, have been prepared recently from material gathered by the Canadian Inventory of Historic Buildings.[5] These are generally well-researched,[6] but since they are internal government documents, they have a limited circulation. With respect to the provincial inventories, one of the few studies which has appeared is *Early Buildings of Manitoba*, published in 1973.[7] Largely the work of student researchers who assisted in the Architectural Survey of Manitoba from 1964 to 1972, it is fundamentally a photographic interpretation rather than a thorough historical discussion of the province's architectural evolution from the age of teepees to the early twentieth century. The main intention of the authors is to stir up public support and government assistance in halting the destruction of Manitoba's remaining old buildings.[8]

On the municipal level, surveys have also become popular in at least two western cities. The City of Victoria's *Heritage Conservation Report*, for example, was prepared by the local Heritage Advisory Committee in 1975.[9] It describes over one hundred structures found in the old community and discloses some of the problems and opportunities involved in historic preservation. Its main purpose is to inform citizens and to promote the retention of the quaint streetscapes that have made Victoria a renowned tourist centre. Information in the report is scant as far as the historian is concerned, but the report does serve an important function in generating further research into the heritage of the community. In Calgary, where progress seemingly lurched forth unobstructed, a similar study of the city's built history was also commissioned by the Planning Department. The "Potential Heritage Sites Evaluation," an unpublished report compiled for local administrators, contains much information on various kinds of buildings erected in the city prior to 1920.[10] Considerable emphasis is given in this study to the physical characteristics of buildings, and currently the City is upgrading its inventory system to include more precise historical information as well.[11]

Generally speaking, such conservation-oriented studies of architecture are restricted in scope. Planners, preservation architects, and other agencies are typically more concerned with the aesthetic component and economic viability of old buildings that they are with their historical significance. This priority is understandable, given their primary goal of enriching the texture of the urban environment. Interestingly, it is often superficial and not of great value to the historian.

During the past few years, broader approaches to the study of western Canadian buildings have been taken by an increasing number of academics and professional researchers. These works have generally been based on the larger premise that architecture is a social, economic, cultural and technological phenomenon, and not merely an aesthetic and material expression. Alan Gowans, one of Canada's foremost architectural historians, has elaborated on this conception.[12] In a public lecture delivered at the Glenbow-Alberta Institute, Gowans argued cogently that one can only understand the significance of styles, and more broadly the meaning of architecture, by examining the social function of buildings in a society. John Lehr's investigations of Ukrainian folk buildings in Alberta, for example, demonstrate very effectively that the cultural values and economic status of Bukowinian and Galician house builders were recorded in the design and construction of their dwellings.[13] A cultural geographer by training, Lehr has documented the building traditions of two distinct ethnic groups in northeastern Alberta based on extensive field work and archival research. Moreover, he has shown that architecture provides a unique source for the study of the social history of a community by noting changes in building forms which coincided with a period of prosperity and cultural assimilation in the region.

Jill Wade's thesis on Red River architecture from the years 1812 to 1870 is another highly interesting inquiry into the nature and methods of folk building.[14] Based primarily on field work, written and pictorial materials, this work explores the design influences and the impact of the local environs on buildings in the Red River settlement.[15] Although Wade is a fine arts student, her observations are not limited to aesthetic trends. Rather, she sees architecture in terms of the social characteristics of the community. The predominance of the *pièce-sur-pièce*, or Hudson's Bay Company, style of log construction is viewed as an indication of the centrality of the fur trade to the settlement for five decades. Similarly, the presence of churches whose stylistic origins can be traced back to British-inspired designs in Québec is seen in terms of the impact of French Canadian population in the area during that period.

Several studies of domestic architecture in a western Canadian urban context have been conducted by Deryck Holdsworth, another geographer. His Master's thesis, an empirical analysis of stylistic preferences in Vancouver housing, represented his first major work on the subject of vernacular architecture.[16] It provided the essential background for a more exploratory paper entitled "House and Home in Vancouver: Images of West Coast Urbanism,

1886-1929," in which the author examines the rationale behind people's choices of house styles.[17] Concentrating on two of the most popular designs evident in the city, the California Bungalow and the Tudor Revival styles, Holdsworth investigates the social values and aspirations of Vancouver's working-class population and upper-class élite, their respective notions of the home environment, and the social significance of their identification with certain architectural images. His aim was to discover the extent to which their choices replicate old preferences and ideas, and the extent to which they signify a rejection of the past. In another essay prepared for Parks Canada's occasional papers series, Holdsworth and co-author G.E. Mills account for the origin, variety and distribution of the B.C. Mills system of prefabricated buildings.[18] Particular attention is given to the ready-made house designs which became the logical choice for many working-class people in Vancouver and across western Canada during the early years of this century. Like other studies undertaken by Holdsworth, this paper sheds a great deal of light on the architectural landscape and nature of the community which was taking shape in Vancouver and the west.

Specific works on Calgary's historic buildings have also begun to appear in recent years. In the past, brief and anecdotal monographs, such as Richard Cunniffe's *Calgary in Sandstone*[19] and Trudy Soby's *A Walk Through Old Calgary* and *Be It Ever So Humble*[20] have been the norm for historical discussion of local architecture. While these studies are quite informative, they tend to focus on the city's oldest buildings, particularly the sandstone structures, and thus present a somewhat sketchy view of Calgary's architectural development. They are helpful, nevertheless, in stimulating public interest, and possibly in motivating more serious investigations of the community's built history.

Of late, more analytical works on Calgary architecture have emerged. Janice Dickin McGinnis, a social historian, has written a concise review of local building activity in "Birth to Boom to Bust: Building in Calgary, 1875-1914."[21] Based largely on research done for Parks Canada's Canadian

Inventory of Historic Buildings, this paper traces construction trends from the settlement's humble origins to the pre-war boom period. It includes much information on Calgary's building industry, examines the importance of several structures to the emerging community, and also considers the special role of various entrepreneurs in the city's growth. The essay is, however, limited by its brevity. Furthermore, it does not specifically deal with such issues as stylistic preferences in Calgary, the physical character of the evolving landscape or the social, demographic and economic forces which shaped building in the city.

Another highly descriptive exposition of local buildings erected in the same extensive period has been presented by Gregory Utas, an architectural historian.[22] Unlike Dickin McGinnis, Utas focusses on Calgary buildings almost exclusively as aesthetic compositions. Starting with an overview of frontier buildings, the author describes the beginnings of sandstone architecture following the famous fire of 1886, which destroyed a substantial portion of the town. He identifies, in a highly theoretical manner, two architectural movements that had emerged by the 1890s: the internal stream, which was essentially experimental and grew out of local environmental conditions and the immediate necessities that were forced on the struggling community; and the colonial stream, which was imitative and sought to transfer design ideas from established centres abroad. Citing numerous examples of these trends, Utas notes that by 1907 the colonial stream had become dominant. In the years leading up to the war, Calgary architecture subsequently entered the mature stage of provincialism, the mainstream of modern design and technology.[23]

Although this study examines Calgary buildings from an interesting perspective, it is thematically narrow. Utas depicts these structures solely in terms of their architectural elements and subjective appeal, and virtually ignores their function in the community. Only superficial treatment has been given to other than aesthetic factors which influenced Calgary buildings. Furthermore, this work surveys only notable commercial and institutional edifices; little is learned about the overall character of the architectural landscape, or of the society which these buildings served.

From this brief summary of secondary literature on western Canadian buildings, it is apparent that a more comprehensive approach to Calgary's buildings is required.[24] The aim of the following book is therefore twofold. First, this study will account for the buildings erected between 1905 and 1914 as visual components of the evolving urban environment. Wherever possible, trends in architectural styling and building construction will be noted. Second, it will explore the social function of these buildings in Calgary. That is, it will attempt to understand the erection of a large number of buildings in terms of the interplay of economic, demographic, social and cultural factors, and to portray changes in the city's self-image which accompanied this, a most profound era of growth.

# Notes

[1] R. Furneaux Jordan, *A Concise History of Western Architecture* (Norwich: Thames and Hudson, 1969; reprint ed., 1975), p. 6.

[2] See H.A. Kalman, "Recent Literature on the History of Canadian Architecture," *Society of Architectural Historians Journal* 31 (December 1972): 315-323, for a more complete commentary on the subject.

[3] *Ibid.* See also R.H. Hubbard, *The Development of Canadian Art* (Ottawa: The National Gallery of Canada, 1963); Thomas Ritchie, *Canada Builds, 1867-1967* (Toronto: University of Toronto Press, 1967); Alan Gowans, *Building Canada: An Architectural History of Canadian Life* (Toronto: Oxford University Press, 1966).

[4] The Canadian Inventory of Historic Buildings represented the first endeavour to compile data on the built heritage of the nation. It was established in 1970 by the National Historic Parks and Sites Branch of Parks Canada, Department of Indian and Northern Affairs. One of its chief

objectives was to conduct a survey of buildings erected in western Canada prior to 1914. At present, a great portion of this work has been completed, and the inventory currently contains information on a total of 200,000 sites across the country. Numerous internal reports have been prepared on the basis of research undertaken in this project, but these studies are not formal publications *per se*. Of the provinces, only Ontario and Alberta have full-fledged inventory programmes which are aimed at compiling detailed architectural and historical information. Québec has a programme as well, but it is more concerned with settlement patterns in the province than with its architectural heritage. Similarly, Manitoba and British Columbia have less ambitious projects, while Saskatchewan is presently in the process of establishing a comprehensive survey that is on par with Alberta's. According to Mark Rasmussen, past Co-ordinator of Alberta Culture's Architectural Inventory, Alberta has the largest provincial survey of all, with over thirty-five thousand sites on file. In existence only since 1976, it has quickly become a vast reservoir of data on buildings erected in the province prior to 1925. Several occasional papers have been commissioned by Alberta Culture, but as yet no actual publications have emerged from the survey itself.

[5] E. Kendal, *The Development of Edmonton and Its Buildings*, Manuscript Report no. 257 (Ottawa: Parks Canada, 1977); E. Mills, *The Early Court Houses of Alberta*, Manuscript Report no. 310 (Ottawa: Parks Canada, 1977); R.R. Rostecki, *The Early Court Houses of Saskatchewan*, Manuscript Report no. 306 (Ottawa: Parks Canada, 1977). These works are available in the library at Parks Canada, Western Regional Office, Calgary.

[6] Kendal's work is somewhat superficial in its description of Edmonton buildings, despite the author's attempt to relate social and economic trends to the city's architecture. Mills's and Rostecki's studies of provincial court houses by comparison, are more analytical in their portrayal of institutional and social development in the prairies.

[7] J. Hockman et al., *Early Buildings of Manitoba* (Winnipeg: Peguis Publishers, 1973).

[8]*Ibid.*, p. i.

[9]City of Victoria Heritage Advisory Committee, *Heritage Conservation Report* (Victoria: City of Victoria, 1975).

[10]City of Calgary Planning Department, "Potential Heritage Sites Evaluation," 4 vols. (Unpublished report prepared by Crothers Pearson Consulting, 1976). Hereafter cited as PHSE.

[11]Under the guidance of the Heritage Planner, several studies of vernacular architecture and urban development have recently been undertaken.

[12] Alan Gowans, "The Architecture of the First and Second British Empires" (Public Lecture, Glenbow-Alberta Institute, March 27, 1979). See also Gowans, "The Evolution of Architectural Styles in Toronto," in *The Canadian City: Essays in Urban History*, ed. A.F.J. Artibise and G.A. Stelter. The Carleton Library Series, no. 109 (Toronto: McClelland and Stewart, 1977), p. 221.

[13]J.C. Lehr, *Ukrainian Vernacular Architecture in Alberta*, Alberta Culture Occasional Papers Series, no. 1 (Edmonton: Alberta Culture Historic Sites Service, 1976), p. 35. See also J.C. Lehr, "Ukrainian Houses in Alberta," *Alberta Historical Review* 21 (Autumn 1973): 9-15; and "Changing Ukrainian House Styles," *Alberta History* 23 (Winter 1975): 25-29.

[14]C.J. Wade, "Red River Architecture, 1812-1870" (Unpublished Master's thesis, University of British Columbia, 1967).

[15]*Ibid.*, p. 3.

[16]D.W. Holdsworth, "Vernacular Forms in an Urban Context: A Preliminary Investigation of Facade Elements in Vancouver Housing" (Unpublished Master's thesis, University of British Columbia, 1971).

[17]D.W. Holdsworth, "House and Home in Vancouver: Images of West Coast Urbanism, 1886-1929," in *The Canadian City*, ed. Artibise and Stelter, pp. 186-211.

[18]D.W. Holdsworth and G.E. Mills, "The B.C. Mills Prefabricated System: The Emergence of Ready-Made Buildings in Western Canada," Canadian Historic Sites

Occasional Papers in Archaeology and History, no. 14 (Ottawa: Parks Canada, 1975).

[19]R.A. Cunniffe, *Calgary in Sandstone* (Calgary: Historical Society of Alberta, 1969).

[20]Trudy Soby, *A Walk Through Old Calgary* (Calgary: Century Calgary Publications, 1974) and *Be It Ever So Humble* (Calgary: Century Calgary Publications, 1975). Another more critical assessment of architectural styles in Calgary has been given by Soby in an unpublished essay which is filed at the Glenbow-Alberta Institute Archives (hereafter cited as GAI). Also in the Archives' manuscript collection is a draft version of a slide show script by Lorne Render, Curator of Art at the Glenbow Museum. This presentation explores the stylistic derivations of especially pre-1900 buildings in Calgary, although in an informal manner.

[21]J.P. Dickin McGinnis, "Birth to Boom to Bust: Building in Calgary, 1875-1914," in *Frontier Calgary: Town, City and Region, 1875-1914*, ed. A.W. Rasporich and H.C. Klassen, (Calgary: McClelland and Stewart West, 1975), pp. 6-19.

[22]G.P. Utas, "Calgary Architecture, 1875-1915" (Unpublished M.E.Des. degree project, University of Calgary, 1975).

[23]*Ibid.*, pp. 22, 24, 25, 42, 72.

[24]Other secondary works which proved insightful with respect to Calgary architecture include: Paul Voisey, "In Search of Wealth and Status: An Economic and Social Study of Entrepreneurs in Early Calgary," in *Frontier Calgary*, ed. Rasporich and Klassen, pp. 221-241; M.L. Foran, "Land Speculation and Urban Development in Calgary, 1884-1912," in *Frontier Calgary*, ed. Rasporich and Klassen, pp. 203-220; and M.L. Foran, *Calgary An Illustrated History*, The History of Canadian Cities Series (Toronto: James Lorimer and Company, Publishers, and the National Museums of Canada, 1978).

# 1.

# Urban Growth and Building Construction in Calgary, 1905–1914

Between 1905 and 1914 Calgary grew phenomenally in population, physical size and economic importance. While the years 1905 through 1909 were characterized by relatively slow growth, the pace of development was quickened to a frenetic level during the boom period of 1909 to 1913. Increasing agricultural production in the immediate hinterland, the promise of the Canadian Northern and Grand Trunk Pacific railways to locate in the city, and later the decision of the Canadian Pacific Railway to erect its enormous western car repair shops at Ogden, all contributed to Calgary's rapid social and economic transformation. During these years the urban landscape was altered drastically. The expenditure of some $40 million in the construction of buildings gave Calgary a new air of modernity and affluence; the last vestiges of the frontier image consequently faded quickly. In addition to providing for the expanding needs of the community, these structures heralded Calgary's emergence as a thriving contemporary of other more established metropolitan centres in the east. In 1913, however, depressed economic conditions throughout the west curtailed the city's explosive rate of growth. With the outbreak of World War I and subsequent losses of manpower and capital, Calgary was brought to a virtual standstill. The towering edifices and urban sprawl created in that time stood as stark reminders of the halcyon days of prosperity and dynamic expansion which ended as abruptly as they had begun.

This chapter will examine various aspects of urban growth in Calgary before the war, particularly the years of the building boom. First, increments in the city's population, patterns of residential, industrial and commercial expansion, the extension of municipal services, and the actual volume of building construction throughout the period will be documented. Next, in order to understand the significance of the buildings erected in this decade properly, attention will be given to the economic circumstances—local and regional—which accounted for Calgary's meteoric rise as a dynamic metropolis. Expanding economic opportunities attracted thousands of immigrants to the city with the result that the demand for public and private buildings of all kinds accelerated dramatically, thus precipitating a building boom. At the same time, it was the excitement of the boom itself that lured countless others to Calgary to take advantage of lucrative investment opportunities in business and real estate.

# Demographic and Physical Growth

In the first fifteen years of the new century, the city's population swelled immensely. In 1901, the *Dominion Census* recorded that 4,091 people were living in Calgary.[1] Five years later, the population reached 11,967,[2] and in the following period of intense immigration, Calgary could boast of 60,502 residents. Yet the most rapid rate of growth was experienced between 1909 and 1913. In those years the city more than doubled its population; according to one estimate, there were 80,851 people in the city in 1913, and upwards of one thousand people moving in each month.[3] This rosy situation was ended, however, by setbacks in the regional economy, unemployment

## Population of Calgary, 1901-1915

| Year | Population or Estimate | Year | Population or Estimate |
|------|------------------------|------|------------------------|
| 1901 | 4,091 | 1909 | 29,265 |
| 1902 | 5,000 | 1910 | 40,000 |
| 1903 | 8,000 | 1911 | 60,502 |
| 1904 | 10,543 | 1912 | 73,759 |
| 1905 | 12,500 | 1913 | 80,851 |
| 1906 | 11,967 | 1914 | 81,161 |
| 1907 | 21,040 | 1915 | 67,504 |
| 1908 | 25,000 | | |

Sources: *The Dominion Census*, 1901, 1906, 1911; *Gronlunds' City Directory*, 1902; *Henderson's Calgary Directory*, 1908, 1910, 1912-1915; *City of Calgary*, 1904-1907, 1910, 1911; *Police Department Records*, 1909

problems and, finally, the outbreak of war in Europe. In 1915, the city's population had fallen well below the figure for 1912.

Ethnically, the dominant group in the city during these spectacular years of growth were the Anglo-Celts. According to the *Dominion Census* of 1911, over 70 percent of the total population of the city were of British descent.[4] It is thus not surprising that Calgary society, particularly members of the city's entrepreneurial and administrative élite, showed a distinct predilection towards British institutions, ideas, and fashions.

The city expanded incredibly in response to population pressure and, by 1909, Calgary covered an area of twelve square miles.[5] Annexations to the municipality in 1910 and 1911 increased this to forty and one-half square miles by 1914.[6] Much of this newly-acquired land was used either for residential or industrial development, commercial activity remaining for the most part in the city's central core near the Canadian Pacific Railway terminal.

While Calgary residents had previously tended to locate close in to their places of employment, it became practical for many to move outward, to more remote, fancifully named suburbs following the completion of the main lines of the city-owned electric street railway in 1909.[7] Suburban land was considerably cheaper and afforded many the opportunity to buy or build their own homes. There were 1,689 dwellings in Calgary in 1901,[8] but with the continuous influx of newcomers and the availability of cheap land in peripheral subdivisions, the construction of single-family homes climbed sharply. By 1911, there were 11,350 dwellings, most of them single-family residences,[9] and in 1911 alone, over 2,000 were built.[10] Calgary was fast gaining a reputation as a city of houses, for residential structures were a dominant feature of the sprawling urban landscape.[11] At the same time, the construction of rental property was keeping pace. Escalating land prices and building costs prohibited many from owning their own homes by the end of the boom. Local investors and other men of means did not hesitate to act in this lucrative situation, since there was no perceptible end to Calgary's growth. Rental property construction soon became significant. Whereas in 1910 there were only sixteen apartment buildings listed in a local directory, by 1913 there were eighty-one.[12]

Accommodation was desperately needed throughout this period, particularly by lower income working-class people. To meet the situation, the city struck an agreement with landowners in east Calgary from whom industrial sites had been purchased in 1911, "to hold the east half of those blocks lying east of city property up to November, 1914 for working men's home sites, to be sold to industrial or manufacturing concerns locating on this property at not more than $100 per 25 -foot lot and to be used for the purpose above mentioned."[13]

The labour force of the manufacturing industries rose from one thousand in 1909[14] to well over four thousand in 1913,[15] as more than sixty factories were established in the same period. Though by no means the only major industry in the city, the CPR repair shops at Ogden were probably the most significant operation in terms of physical dimensions and overall contribution to local population growth. It was estimated by the *Albertan* that with 2,000 employees at the shops which occupied a total area of 360 acres,[16] no less than 10,000 people would be added to the community.[17] Other large manufacturing complexes in Calgary included the Pioneer Tractor Company, Dominion Bridge Company, P. Burns Company abattoir, Calgary Brewing and Malting Company, and numerous flour milling operations, lumber yards and ceramic plants. These and other facilities accounted for a great proportion of land used in the city's southeastern subdivisions of Mills Estates, Inglewood, Manchester and Ogden, and indirectly for the location of some of Calgary's notable working-class residential districts.

Commercial development, although restricted essentially to the downtown core, was highly active as well. In 1906, there were sixty-four wholesale houses clustered around the CPR right-of-way.[18] At the apex of the boom there were 160.[19] Business blocks continued to be erected for retail purposes and office space eastward and westward along

Eighth Avenue, down First Street West, on Seventeenth Avenue Southwest and Tenth Street North. in 1909, fully fifty-two blocks were built,[20] while in 1912, 109 were constructed.[21] Banks similarly proliferated. In 1906, there were a dozen in the city,[22] by 1914, twenty-seven branches were doing business locally, many in new, affluently styled buildings which spoke of the city's confident position in the financial world.[23]

Another aspect of Calgary's growth in this period can be seen in the extension of municipal services to the burgeoning community. Having decided that publicly-owned utilities were in the best interests of its citizens, the city in 1900 purchased from a private company a water works system, which was then modernized. Over the course of the next dozen years, an electrical light and power system, street railway, asphalt paving plant, sewage system and numerous other ventures were undertaken.[24] In 1906, local residents were proud of the fact that the business section had sidewalks and that there were thirteen miles of improved streets and four parks in the city.[25] By the end of the decade under study, there were almost 150 miles of water mains and 188 miles of sewers in the city,[26] most of which had been rapidly constructed in the boom era. The rationale for these expenditures was simple and straightforward—without services, Calgary could not compete with other western urban centres in attracting immigrants, investors and industries. The creation of an advanced physical environment vis-à-vis transportation corridors, sanitation facilities, and other modern amenities was not only conducive to healthy, moral living in an urban setting, but it was also absolutely vital in building Calgary's reputation as a modern, twentieth-century city interested in the general welfare of its citizens, both corporate and private.

Probably the best indicators of Calgary's growth between 1905 and 1914 can be seen in the figures for building construction. As a result of unceasing migration to the city, existing private and public facilities were stretched beyond their capacity to meet the needs of the populace. The requirement for residences, commercial structures, schools, churches, hospitals, administrative buildings, meeting halls and other buildings multiplied. Fortunately, buoyant economic circumstances and a ready supply of labour favoured the emergence of a bustling construction industry. There were fluctuations in building activity in the first five years of the period, notably in 1908, owing to financial stringencies across Canada and elsewhere,[27] but on the whole, construction figures demonstrated a steady increase. The years 1910, 1911, and 1912 showed a spectacular rise in building construction of all kinds, due primarily to the heightened rate of population growth in the city and, secondarily, to real estate speculation, commercial expansion and the proposed extension of numerous rail lines to Calgary. Prospects for another record-breaking year were extremely good at the outset of 1913; however, the situation was darkened by the spectre of an economic recession several months later. Local boosters were willing to overlook the somewhat dismal showing of 1913, since the total value of work done was well above the figures for 1910. In 1914, it was rosily

## Building Permits and Values in Calgary, 1905-1915

| Year | Permits Issued | Value ($) |
|------|----------------|-----------|
| 1905 | — | 838,829 |
| 1906 | — | 1,097,136 |
| 1907 | 605 | 2,094,264 |
| 1908 | 423 | 1,004,520 |
| 1909 | 777 | 2,420,450 |
| 1910 | 1,499 | 5,589,594 |
| 1911 | 2,619 | 12,907,638 |
| 1912 | 3,483 | 20,394,220 |
| 1913 | 2,078 | 8,619,653 |
| 1914 | 1,255 | 3,425,350 |
| 1915 | 272 | 150,500 |

Source:    *City of Calgary Municipal Manual*, 1915, p. 172;
           *Henderson's Calgary Directory*, 1922.

predicted that with oil production at Turner Valley there would be a healthy revival in local construction and investment. The outbreak of World War I vaporized these hopes, and building activity consequently dropped off. By 1915, the level of construction in the city plummetted to less than one-fifth of what it had been in 1905.

# Changing Economic Conditions and the Boom Period

Calgary's phenomenal growth in the years between 1905 and 1915 was influenced essentially by two factors: the expansion of economic opportunities on a local and regional level and the coming of millions of immigrants to the western plains. The prospect of free land was highly appealing; so, too, was the prospect of profitable employment of capital. Continued railway expansion subsequently opened up vast tracts of land for settlement, thus marking the end of the golden age of ranching in western Canada. The development of large-scale irrigation schemes and other farming improvements reaffirmed the completeness of the west's changed role. In this process of economic transformation, Calgary emerged as a successful metropolitan centre with a renewed sense of purpose. The flurry of building and speculation which accompanied this transition provides hard evidence of rejuvenated faith in the city's ascendant economic status and promise for the future.

Calgary rose to commercial dominance early owing to its fortuitous position on the CPR mainline and its proximity to southern Alberta ranches. For ranching establishments, the community immediately became a geographic locus providing transportation, marketing and social services.[28] In spite of the British embargo on Canadian cattle in 1892, the stock-raising industry thrived in the foothills country, thus bringing a great deal of business to Calgary. Beef requirements increased substantially with the opening of mines in Kootenay-Crowsnest district and the swift rise of Canadian cities.[29] In the meantime, ranching had a direct impact on Calgary's development. As well as encouraging the establishment of subsidiary industries such as meat-packing plants and saddleries, some of the first major capital investment in real estate, business blocks and manufacturing came from prominent individuals in ranching. Pat Burns, William Roper Hull, Alfred E. Cross, Ezra Riley, Fred Stimson and others actively diversified their financial interests in Calgary, thus reinforcing the city's function as a regional hub.[30]

It was, however, after ranching had subsided that Calgary experienced its most dynamic growth. Ranching dwindled because of low prices for livestock, drought, and bitter winters in 1906/07 and 1911/12.[31] At the same time, the application of improved dry-land farming techniques, the development of fast-maturing hard spring wheat, and the continued expansion of the CPR, and later the CNR and GTP, extended the domain of the wheat economy across the Canadian prairies. By 1912, there were indications of a new order of things in Calgary. In that year, the first Stampede was organized to commemorate the passing of a unique way of life in western Canada. The year also signalled the zenith of homesteading activity on the prairies and the peak of the building boom in Calgary.[32]

According to V.C. Fowke, the establishment of the wheat economy "required the assembly in the prairie provinces of a massive structure of capital equipment without which the large-scale production and marketing of wheat would have been impossible."[33] Farm buildings, machinery, tools, household furnishings, grain elevators, warehouses, stores, and rail lines were all needed by the millions of settlers who streamed onto the plains to take up the challenge of the agricultural frontier. As dictated by the National Policy, products and lumber were supplied by central Canadian manufacturers and west coast millmen via the Canadian Pacific Railway. The opening of the wheat frontier was not only a boon to industry, but was of sufficient magnitude to integrate and vitalize the entire Canadian economy at the time.[34] Billions of dollars poured into the country from abroad to finance western expansion and industrial development.[35] Since Calgary was situated on the CPR route and had early demonstrated its primacy as a regional centre, the city was assured of a significant share of the profits arising from this economic transformation.

Homesteading activity on the prairies was most
concentrated between the years 1909 and 1912. During that
period the driest zone of the plains—the area between
Calgary and Moose Jaw—was opened for homestead and
pre-emption entry.[36] Better than average rainfall resulted in
good yields for recently arrived farmers; nevertheless, it
was well known that parts of the area were almost too arid
for consistently successful farming. To remedy a potentially
difficult situation, the CPR committed itself to the
construction of a vast irrigation system stretching from
Bassano to Medicine Hat which would bring hundreds of
thousands of acres of land into agricultural production.[37]
According to the *Albertan*, the project was to be one of the
largest in the entire world.[38] In addition to supplying
materials for the $30 million work, Calgary became the
headquarters for the administration of these irrigated
lands, and in fact for the whole western division of the

## Building Permits and Values by Months,

| | 1909 | | 1910 | |
|---|---|---|---|---|
| | Permits | Values | Permits | Values |
| January | 18 | $ 21,650 | 49 | $ 106,500 |
| February | 34 | 78,050 | 55 | 169,800 |
| March | 54 | 94,900 | 148 | 415,800 |
| April | 55 | 174,150 | 189 | 603,930 |
| May | 66 | 377,650 | 156 | 525,060 |
| June | 65 | 202,710 | 162 | 573,846 |
| July | 88 | 182,280 | 133 | 520,098 |
| August | 69 | 242,175 | 124 | 449,998 |
| September | 112 | 280,738 | 100 | 720,872 |
| October | 111 | 403,050 | 165 | 568,290 |
| November | 69 | 211,550 | 158 | 590,604 |
| December | 37 | 151,550 | 80 | 354,300 |

Sources: *Calgary Daily Herald*, January 4, 1910, April 29, May 31, July 20,
August 2, 1912; *Morning Albertan*, January 4, 1912;
*Calgary News Telegram*, January 16, 1913;

CPR's land, resources and transportation. The city thus emerged stronger than ever, with more opportunities for employment, investment and commercial expansion.

Calgary's role as an important transportation, wholesaling and manufacturing centre was further underscored by the announcement of railway extensions in the city. In February 1909, the *Albertan* exclaimed that nine new lines were heading for Calgary, all supposed to be completed by 1912.[39] Every line was seen as opening up valuable lands hitherto inaccessible to settlers.[40] Coalfields in the vicinity provided another incentive for expansion. Although all of the projected routes were not built, the excitement generated by the mushrooming economy was sufficient to sustain a boom period in the city. This development conveniently coincided with the arrival of myriads of settlers onto the plains, the patiently awaited fruit of the federal government's immigration scheme.

## 1909-1912

| | 1911 Permits | Values | 1912 Permits | Values |
|---|---|---|---|---|
| January | 37 | $ 296,040 | unknown | $ 381,384 |
| February | 110 | 332,660 | " | 938,724 |
| March | 219 | 1,012,260 | " | 1,086,210 |
| April | 320 | 1,127,256 | " | 1,708,380 |
| May | 306 | 3,616,812 | " | 2,215,392 |
| June | 314 | 4,826,220 | " | 2,210,580 |
| July | 214 | 817,980 | " | 1,350,516 |
| August | 286 | 927,540 | " | 2,799,280 |
| September | 268 | 903,210 | " | 4,170,360 |
| October | 288 | 803,160 | " | 1,595,490 |
| November | 188 | 545,340 | " | 1,903,944 |
| December | 110 | 698,160 | " | 1,033,560 |

*City of Calgary Municipal Manual*, 1915;
*Labour Gazette*, October, December, 1912, January, 1913.

The building boom era, which started part way through 1909 and reached a crescendo in 1912, was fundamentally a response to enhanced opportunities for capital investment, business and industrial expansion and the employment of labour, as presented by the opening of the wheat frontier. Over the course of these four years, nearly ten thousand buildings were erected, worth an estimated $50 million.[41] As the population swelled and the social nature of the city changed, the need for buildings of all kinds intensified. Each year witnessed the construction of new residences, public and institutional buildings, facilities for expanding community services, and commercial and industrial structures. Generally speaking, Calgary buildings tended year by year to be bigger and more functional, utilizing up-to-date construction techniques and materials, and aimed increasingly at providing safety, health, comfort, and convenience. Architects, contractors and builders in the city brought local development progressively closer in step with the advanced aesthetic and technological trends in the United States and Great Britain.

Financing for local construction and development was made possible through both foreign and Canadian capitalists.[42] As a result of favourable accounts of business advancement in Bradstreet's report[43] and the mass circulation of promotional literature across North America and overseas, the city attracted considerable attention to itself. The *Herald* applauded the influx of enormous amounts of money as "unmistakable evidence of the confidence of capital in Calgary investment and in the immediate growth of the city into a great center."[44] English investment was particularly strong throughout the boom period, due, perhaps, to the renewed zeal of imperial denizens seeking to revive Great Britain's fading economy in the face of mounting competition from Germany and the United States.[45] By the same token, Canadian investment was also heavy as many seized the opportunity to build the country, and with it amass their own personal fortunes.

Increased investment activity pushed Calgary into a period of frenzied real estate speculation. Land and buildings were rapidly bought and sold in anticipation of overnight profits. Values for real estate climbed steadily during the first months of the boom; at the outset of 1909 residential lots could be purchased for $100 to $120, while retail lots 25 feet by 140 feet could be had for $100 to $800 per front foot.[46] Several months later, a lot on Eighth Avenue was sold to an Englishman for an incredible $1,200 per front foot.[47] Near the end of 1909, prices began to skyrocket. In November, F.E. Osborne paid $1,750 per front foot for land on Eighth Avenue, at that time the highest price ever paid for property in the central business district.[48] In 1913, the Canada Life Assurance Company paid $2,000 per front foot for its site on Eighth Avenue and Second Street West, and the Royal Bank paid an astronomical $4,000 per front foot for the old Hudson's Bay Company store on Eighth Avenue and Centre Street.[49] Residential lots also appreciated substantially. According to one realtor, property in 1911 varied from $200 to $2,250 per lot depending on the closeness to the Post Office.[50] Business in real estate proceeded briskly at this time. In 1909, there were sixty-three realtors in the city,[51] and by 1912, there were around two thousand.[52] Rising prices and active business were important to the city, as they attracted further investment and fuelled the fires of the building boom.

The upswing in Calgary construction began in 1909. Despite sluggish economic conditions in 1908,[53] the city was able to bounce back to its former vital self. The production of the finest crop ever seen in Alberta in the autumn of 1908,[54] followed by the announcement of railway expansion into Calgary, changed the direction of the winds of fortune for local entrepreneurs. During 1909, nearly $2.5 million—over double the value for 1908—was spent in the construction of 52 business blocks, 15 warehouses, 4 schools, 5 elevators and grain tanks and 617 private residences.[55] With growing opportunities for commercial development, low prices for building materials, easier terms for borrowing money and rising real estate values, Calgary buildings became a seemingly secure investment.[56] Structures which were either begun or completed included the Tees and Persse warehouse, the Ashdown warehouse, and the Fairey apartment and business block, each worth $40,000; the Samis Block worth

$55,000; the Blow Block, worth $45,000; the Ellis and Grogan warehouse, the International Harvester Building, St. Mary's School, the Salvation Army Building, the Carnegie Library and the new Riverside Lumber Company Factory.[57] The crowning spectacle of all was the Grain Exchange Building, Calgary's first modern reinforced concrete skyscraper, worth $150,000.[58] Yet, the year was not without its disappointments. City Hall remained incomplete even though it was started in 1907; serious troubles were brewing between the municipal government and architect William Dodd over delays and spiralling costs.[59]

Building activity accelerated during the next year. Figures for construction in 1910 reached more than twice the high mark of 1909. It was anticipated that within the year, new wings would be added to both the Holy Cross Hospital and the CPR depot, and that freight sheds and stations would be built for the long-awaited Canadian Northern and Grand Trunk Pacific railways.[60] Numerous impressive structures were also planned, including the new Court House, the Dominion Bank, Mount Royal College, the King George Hotel and the Devenish Apartments.[61] In all, some 14 business blocks, 16 warehouses, 9 terraces and apartment blocks, 5 schools, over 1,100 private residences and many other buildings were built.[63]

The following year was expected to be even better for construction, and it was, as more than $12.5 million was spent on assorted buildings. Two works accounted for a significant proportion of this sum: the Hudson's Bay Company retail store and the CPR's Palliser Hotel, both started in 1911, were initially estimated to be worth a fantastic $1.5 million each.[64] Calgary's City Hall was finally completed that year after William Dodd, the architect, was fired and more money was obtained in a civic plebiscite.[65] The Carnegie Library, another outstanding project, was also brought to completion although the opening date was pushed ahead to early January of the new year.[66] The enormous Devenish Apartments and the Underwood Block were similarly finished, while work was commenced on the Beveridge, Bruner and Maclean Blocks, the CPR Colonization Building, the Fire Department Headquarters,

Argyle Court, First Baptist Church, the Molsons' Bank, Pryce-Jones Company department store and other structures.[67] In addition, another thirteen schools were worked on, including at least seven temporary cottage structures, to meet the pressing public educational needs of the expanding community.[68] Residential construction continued to be a major factor in 1911, especially in outlying districts, with 2,054 private dwellings being built across the city.[69] In the downtown area, the growth of the commercial section caused problems for long-time residents who began to express grievances regarding the uncontrolled erection of business premises next to their homes.[70] It was immediately apparent from this situation that Calgary was beginning to outgrow its small city character, and that a more ambitious scheme for ordering the physical environment was called for.

The year 1912 proved to be the most spectacular of all in the boom period. A total of 3,483 permits were issued by the city building inspector worth in excess of $20 million. Among the more important buildings worked on were the extensive CPR repair shops which cost about $2.5 million; Knox Presbyterian Church; the Burns Building; The Travellers Building; the Harvetta, Graves and Mackie Blocks; the Connaught Apartments; the Canada Life Assurance Building; the Herald Building; the McDougall and Foster warehouse; and King George, Sunalta, Ramsay and King Edward schools. Altogether, 109 business buildings, 52 warehouses and factories, 12 schools, 3 government buildings, 12 churches, 44 apartments and hotels, 4 firehalls, 2,416 residences plus numerous other structures were built in 1912.[72] The year's accomplishments were staggering indeed. The *Herald* was exuberant: "Calgary has eclipsed every known record in building growth, during 1912, of any city of its comparable size in the history of the world."[73] In an attempt to grasp the full meaning of the feat, the *Herald* described the achievement within the more realistic context of western Canada.

> *Calgary built more in dollars and cents than*
> *Edmonton, Moose Jaw and Medicine Hat*
> *combined . . . To simplify the statement, Calgary*

> *has built more in any one month than Lethbridge built in the entire year. During the month of October, Calgary's building permits were nearly twice as much as Medicine Hat for the entire year. To define a comparison to a day, Calgary has built as much in one day as Portage la Prairie built in the entire year.*[74]

Aside from the sheer volume of construction carried on, certain advances were made with respect to the organization and management of the city's evolving urban environment. The adoption of a rigorous and progressive building code,[75] together with the establishment of the City Planning Commission in October 1912,[76] signified that the local government was dedicated to the safety, health and convenience of its residents, and not to unqualified and incoherent expansion. The city was hence guaranteed recognition as an enlightened community, a leader in the field of civic development.

With the continued influx of a thousand people a month and no end in sight to the building bonanza, it was confidently predicted early in the new year that 1913 would yield even greater results. E.A. Dagg, President of the Calgary Board of Trade, offered local residents a highly optimistic synopsis of future growth in a letter to the *News Telegram.*

> *To Calgarians the future is indeed bright. Soon the Panama Canal will be opened and that event should enormously benefit the entire west, Calgary in particular. As well, more people continue to come in and with more people comes more prosperity. The prosperity of western Canada should continue to increase until all arable land is under cultivation. By that time we will have big cities, with big factories, full of prosperous happy people and there will be tens of thousands of farmers . . . In the days to come this should be the modern Utopia . . .*[77]

As well, the *Albertan* projected that the population would reach one hundred thousand and that at least $25 million would be spent on new facilities by the end of the year.[78]

As support for this prognostication, the *Albertan* noted that Tregillus Clay Products, Pioneer Tractor Company and Riverside Lumber Company were planning to augment their employment substantially, and that the opening of the Panama Canal would divert a great deal more business to the city.[79] The announcement by Sir James Lougheed, the Conservative Party leader in the Senate, that the Dominion government proposed to build a new Post Office, customs warehouse, immigration building and possibly an armoury over the year seemed to reaffirm the prophecies of growth.[80] So, too, did the continued work on Calgary's most striking buildings: the Hudson's Bay Company store, Knox Presbyterian Church, the Canada Life Assurance Building, the Burns Building, Grace Presbyterian Church, the Calgary Herald Building, the Calgary Furniture Company store, and other fine structures.[81] However, with the sudden slump in the western Canadian economy which hit Calgary in July,[82] building and real estate activity tapered off. Once again investment capital became extremely difficult to obtain,further hampering construction. The situation was complicated by the fact that municipal finances were in an appalling tangle in 1913. During the previous year, public expenditures had escalated by 75 percent, which necessitated the raising of the mill rate from 12.5 to 18.75, the greatest jump for a single year in the city's history.[83] With the extra burden of a fiscal deficit, certain public works such as a new Post Office[84] and Thomas Mawson's grandiose proposal for a comprehensive city plan were stalled. In spite of these troubles, optimism was maintained, if guarded. The *Albertan* assured citizens that there was no cause for alarm, citing Calgary's magnificent manufacturing and business record for the year as evidence of flourishing circumstances,[83] while the *News Telegram* pointed to an impressive array of buildings under consideration to indicate continued progress.[86] The year 1912 was simply written off as an anomaly, a stupendous achievement impossible to repeat in 1913 or any other year, at least until the city had a population of 250,000.[87]

The disappointment of 1913 was not all that serious

considering that the value of construction and the number
of permits issued was well above the figures for 1910.
Nevertheless, it was strongly hoped that with the beginning
of oil production in the Turner Valley field, 1914 would
witness a return to high levels of prosperity and the end of
financial stringency in Calgary.[88] This, unfortunately, did
not prove to be the case. If anything, the oil fields diverted
investment away from the city, forcing a crisis in local
construction. The building industry, unable to survive the
cut-backs in development which began midway through
1913 began to lay off massive numbers of workers.[89]
Agricultural expansion in western Canada had ended; with
the stabilization of production and a drop in grain prices,
the opportunities for capital investment dwindled.[90]
Calgary, as a regional supply, service and transportation
centre, thus tasted the bitter experience of severe
economic recession. Finally, with Canada's entry into
World War I in August and the subsequent removal of a
significant portion of the labour force and investment
money from the local scene, all possible hope of a recovery
by the city was destroyed.

\* \* \*

Between 1905 and 1914, Calgary's urban landscape was
utterly transformed by the dual forces of capitalism and
modernity. As one local booster observed:

> Where a few years ago were bare hills and bald-
> headed prairie . . . are now such beautiful
> suburbs as Bowness, Mount Royal, Elbow Park,
> Elboya, Glencoe and Rosedale . . . Calgary in
> recent years has shown the most phenomenal
> growth of any city on the American continent in
> the same space of time. Million dollar hotels have
> replaced the frontier saloons, million dollar
> department stores have replaced the fur trading
> posts . . .[91]

The construction of thousands of new buildings within a
few short years signified several important changes in the
character of the community. First, the buildings declared
Calgary's emergence as a dominant metropolitan force in

western Canada. With the rapid settlement of nearby farming lands and the extension of railway lines across the plains, a multitude of new buildings were erected to facilitate the city's economic development as a vital supply and service depot, administrative headquarters and industrial centre. Second, the buildings demonstrated that in this era of unprecedented prosperity Calgary had entered into the mainstream of modern architectural design. The use of concrete, steel and other industrially produced materials and the implementation of the latest construction techniques showed that, with respect to buildings, Calgary was quickly becoming a counterpart of larger, more mature urban centres across the continent. Third, these new structures reflected a shift in social attitudes in the city. The frontier image, which had been perpetuated during the golden age of ranching, was swiftly displaced as soaring skyscrapers, opulent public buildings and myriads of mass-produced residences were constructed. These impressive edifices became symbols of a modern, fast-paced and thoroughly urban society that was emerging in Calgary during this decade of phenomenal growth.

The buildings erected in the period 1905 to 1914, particularly those constructed during the boom years, were therefore of great worth to the city of Calgary. As well as providing accommodation for residents, businesses, institutions, industries and essential services, they gave the city a progressive, modern appearance. The grandeur, beauty and prestige which they imparted to the urban environment also filled Calgarians with a deep sense of civic pride. In a time of intense inter-urban rivalry, they supplied Calgary's many boosters with highly visible examples of Calgary's ascendancy as a vibrant regional centre, and furthermore proved useful in attracting the attention of investors to the city's vast economic potential.

# Notes

[1] See *Census of Population and Agriculture of the North-West Provinces*, 1906, table 9, p. 101.

[2] *Ibid.*

[3] *Henderson's Calgary Directory*, 1913 (hereafter cited as *Henderson's Directory*); and *The Story of Calgary-Alberta-Canada. Progress — Resources — Opportunities* (Calgary: n.pub., 1914.)

[4] *Census of Canada*, 1911, vol. 2, table 14, p. 373.

[5] *The Morning Albertan*, special edition, March 1, 1909 (hereafter cited as *Albertan*).

[6] In 1910 the city limits were extended to include Township 24, Range 1, West of the Fifth Meridian. Further extension in 1911 included the northern half of Sections 25, 26, and 34 of Township 23, Range 1, West of the Fifth Meridian; and Sections 28 and 33 of Township 23, Range 29, West of the Fourth Meridian. *City of Calgary Municipal Manual*, 1914, pp. 28-29 (hereafter cited as *Municipal Manual*).

[7] See M.L. Foran, "Land Speculation and Urban Development: Calgary 1884-1912," in *Frontier Calgary*, ed. Rasporich and Klassen (Calgary: McClelland and Stewart West, 1975), pp. 207-209.

[8] *Census of Canada*, 1911, vol. 1, table 11, p. 531.

[9] *Ibid.*

[10] *Albertan*, January 4, 1912.

[11] *Albertan*, February 28, 1911.

[12] *Henderson's Directory*, 1910, and *Tregillus-Thompson Greater Calgary Directory*, 1913 (hereafter cited as *Tregillus-Thompson Directory*).

[13] *Municipal Manual*, 1913, pp. 47-48.

[14] *Albertan*, special edition, March 1, 1909.

[15] *Calgary Board of Trade Annual Report*, 1913, President's Address, p. 9.

[16] *Tregillus-Thompson Directory*, 1913, p. 119.

[17] *Albertan*, January 1, 1913; and February 28, 1912.

[18] *The Calgary Daily Herald*, April 11, 1906 (hereafter cited as *Herald*); and *Calgary Alberta 1906* (Calgary: Dawson Publisher, 1906).

[19]*Municipal Manual*, 1913.

[20]*Herald*, January 4, 1910.

[21]*Henderson's Directory*, 1913, p. 147.

[22]*Herald*, April 11, 1906.

[23]*Municipal Manual*, 1914.

[24]*Municipal Manual*, 1916, p. 16.

[25]*Henderson's Directory*, 1906, pp. 199-200.

[26]*Municipal Manual*, 1914, pp. 162-65, 215-19.

[27]*Herald*, January 2, 1909.

[28]See L.G. Thomas, "The Rancher and the City: Calgary and the Cattlemen," *Transactions of the Royal Society of Canada* 6 , Series 4, Section 2 (June 1968), pp. 203-215. See also David H. Breen, "The Canadian West and the Ranching Frontier, 1875-1922" (Unpublished Ph.D. dissertation, The University of Alberta, 1972).

[29]See C.M. McInnes, *In the Shadow of the Rockies* (London: Rivingtons, 1930). See also Simon Evans, "The Passing of a Frontier: Ranching in the Canadian West, 1886-1912" (Unpublished Ph.D. dissertation, The University of Calgary, 1976).

[30]See Paul Voisey, "In Search of Wealth and Status: An Economic and Social Study of Entrepreneurs in Early Calgary," in *Frontier Calgary*, ed. Rasporich and Klassen, pp. 221-241. See also Max Foran, *Calgary An Illustrated History* (Toronto: James Lorimer and Company, Publishers, and the National Museum of Man, 1978), Chapters One and Two.

[31]See *Albertan*, January 16, 1909.

[32]Evans, "The Passing of a Frontier," p. 34; A.A. Lupton, "Cattle Ranching in Alberta, 1874-1910: Its Evolution and Migration," *Alberta Geographer* 3 (1966-67): 55-58.

[33]V.C. Fowke, *The National Policy and the Wheat Economy* (Toronto: University of Toronto Press, 1957), pp. 71-72.

[34]*Ibid.*, pp. 71, 72, 82.

[35] *Ibid.*, also *Herald*, May 2, 1910, editorial.

[36] *Ibid.*, pp. 72-73, 77.

[37] *Henderson's Alberta Directory*, 1914; Max Foran, *Calgary An Illustrated History*, p. 70; *Albertan*, February 28, 1910, "Advantages of Irrigation — What It Means," "Famous Bow River Valley Irrigation Area," and "Bassano a Busy Town in Irrigation."

[38] *Albertan*, February 25, 1910, "Magnitude of CPR Irrigation Project."

[39] *Albertan*, February 12, 1909.

[40] *Ibid.*, editorial.

[41] These numbers are based on figures for building permits issued for 1909 through part of 1913, and on their estimated value. The actual value of building costs is not readily available. However, in keeping with the advice of Building Inspectors Harrison and Walshaw, a rough figure may be obtained by adding 20 percent to estimated values, as builders tended to underestimate construction costs when applying for permits. See the annual reports of the building inspectors; for example, *Herald*, January 4, 1910.

[42] See H.L. MacLeod, "Properties, Investors and Taxes: A Study of Calgary Real Estate Investment, Municipal Finances and Property Tax Arrears, 1911-1919" (Unpublished Master's thesis, The University of Calgary, 1977), Appendix F for details on selected investment companies involved in Calgary property investment.

[43] *Albertan*, February 15, 1909.

[44] *Herald*, May 31, 1911.

[45] One notable Englishman, John Hextall, came to Calgary in 1908 with the idea of investing in suitable property. He became enthralled with the natural beauties of the land west of Calgary known as Bowness and later planned to build a number of stately English vernacular-styled houses there and open the general area for residential development. Hextall returned to England where he captured the interest of investors by forming the Bowness Land Development Company. In 1912, he built a club

house and golf course overlooking the development where he entertained wealthy English gentlemen who ventured forth to inspect the sites. A water tower, power plant and bridge were also built at Hextall's expense in an effort to attract investment. Unfortunately, following these improvements Hextall died, and his grandiose plans were never realized on their intended scale. See Dorothy Nielsen, "Bowness," in *Communities of Calgary—From Scattered Towns to a Major City* (Calgary: Century Calgary Publications, 1975), pp. 13-17. See also *Herald*, July 15, 1912, advertisement for Bowness.

[46]*Albertan*, March 1, 1909, "One Thousand Facts About Calgary."

[47]*Albertan*, June 2, 1909.

[48]*Herald*, November 5, 1909.

[49]*The Story of Calgary* (Calgary: The 75th Anniversary edition of the *Herald*, 1950), p. 54.

[50]*Herald*, May 25, 1911; see map for Astley and Shackle advertisement.

[51]*Herald*, June 26, 1909.

[52]*Herald*, January 30, 1912.

[53]See *Albertan*, January 16, 1909, Board of Trade Report.

[54]*Ibid.*

[55]*Herald*, January 4, 1910.

[56]*Ibid.*

[57]*Albertan*, February 28, 1910, p. 69; *Herald*, January 20, August 14, 1909.

[58]*Albertan*, February 28, 1910, p. 69.

[59]See *Herald*, March 20, 1909; April 16, 1909, editorial; April 20, 1909; *Albertan*, May 20, 1909; May 27, 1909.

[60]*Albertan*, February 28, 1910, p. 69.

[61]*Albertan*, February 28, 1911. The Court House was not actually started until 1912. See Chapter 3.

[62]*Ibid.* March and November were exceedingly mild

months. See also *Albertan*, March 22, 1910.

[63] *Ibid.*

[64] *Herald*, January 3, 1912.

[65] *Herald*, June 2, 1911.

[66] *Herald*, January 2, 1912.

[67] *Herald*, June 30, 1911; *Albertan*, February 28, 1911; *The Calgary News Telegram*, February 2, 1912, and February 23, 1912 (hereafter cited as *News Telegram*); *Albertan*, April 27, 1911; *Herald*, January 10, 1912.

[68] *Albertan*. February 28, 1912.

[69] *Albertan*, January 4, 1912.

[70] *Herald*, January 13, 1911.

[71] *Herald*, May 10, 1912.

[72] *Ibid.*

[73] *Herald*, January 11, 1913.

[74] *Ibid.*

[75] *Albertan*, February 28, 1913.

[76] *Tregillus-Thompson Directory*, 1913, p. 136.

[77] *News Telegram*, January 2, 1913.

[78] *Albertan*, January 1, 1913.

[79] *Ibid.*

[80] *Ibid.*

[81] *The 100,000 Manufacturing, Building and Wholesale Book Edition* (Calgary: The Morning Albertan, 1914), advertisement by Fyshe, McNeil, Martin, Trainer, General Contractors, p. 56; *Albertan*, August 9, 1913; *Herald*, February 1, 1913.

[82] *Herald*, January 1, 1914. See John Thompson, *The Harvests of War — The Prairie West, 1914-1918* (Toronto: McClelland and Stewart Limited, 1978), pp. 13-14.

[83] *Albertan*, January 8, 1913. See MacLeod, "Properties,

Investors and Taxes," 1977, Table 11.2, p. 10.

[84]*Albertan*, July 3, 1913, editorial.

[85]*Ibid.*

[86]*News Telegram*, August 9, 1913.

[87]*Albertan*, July 3, 1913.

[88]*Albertan*, January 1, 1914.

[89]See *Herald*, October 20, 1916. See also S.J. and H.S. Ferns, *Eighty-Five Years in Canada* (Winnipeg: Queenston House Publishers, 1978) for an autobiographical account of an individual who was employed in the building industry in Calgary during this early period. S.J. Ferns came to Calgary from London, Ontario, in 1909 to make his fortune in the boom. He and his partner operated a successful bricklaying company and speculated in the local real estate market. But with the sudden and unforeseeable shift in the city's economy in 1913, Ferns lost all of his investments as well as his job. His story is typical of thousands who came west in those years and were victimized by the pre-war economic collapse.

[90]Thompson, *The Harvests of War*, pp. 13-14.

[91]*The Story of Calgary-Alberta-Canada, Progress — Resources — Opportunities.*

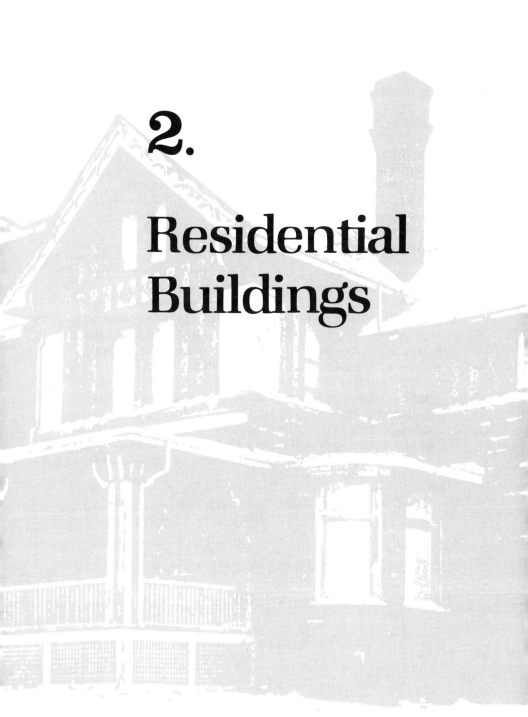

# 2.

# Residential Buildings

One could easily have walked across Calgary in a few short hours in 1905, but by 1914 the city had doubled in size with the incorporation of several villages and vast stretches of surrounding prairie. Extensive as was the geographic expansion of Calgary, the increase in the local population was of greater significance. Entrepreneurs, lured by the seemingly infinite potential of the region, poured their capital resources and experience into the development of business, industry and real estate within the community. Following their lead, workers came in droves as opportunities for employment rapidly multiplied. Thousands more were drawn to the city to supply necessary goods and services. The net result was the transformation of Calgary into an energetic regional metropolis, a modern centre of trade and commerce, industry, transportation, administration and social services.

Because of accelerating demographic pressure, the demand for accommodation in the city constantly outstripped the supply. In no previous era had there ever been a surplus of dwellings; consequently, newly-arrived settlers were faced with a serious housing shortage at the beginning of the decade. Those who had a great deal of money, or access to it, had little difficulty in finding homes. Many, in fact, took advantage of land and labour prices, which were low by eastern Canadian and British standards, to build enormous estates. But those without capital, by far the vast majority of local residents, were hard hit by the lack of houses either for sale or for rent at an affordable price, and were forced to live in tents and shacks. After 1908, however, the availability of mortgage and loan money on easy terms, together with slowly rising wages for labour, tended to ameliorate the situation. Easy terms of purchase and financing enabled many to acquire their own homes. At the same time, the opening of new subdivisions in the city flooded the real estate market with inexpensive land which helped, for a short period, to keep residential lots within the means of a large percentage of the working-class population. Calgary consequently experienced a dramatic surge in residential building. Between 1909 and 1913, the period that the boom was in full swing, a total of 10,456 building permits were issued in the city; of that number, an estimated 7,747 were for residences (see p. 59). Dwelling construction thus not only met a pressing need in the community, but also gave employment to thousands of Calgary tradesmen, and helped immensely in sustaining buoyant conditions in the local economy.

In this chapter, a number of aspects of residential buildings from the period 1905 to 1914 will be discussed. First, the homes of Calgary's entrepreneurial élite will be examined in terms of their exterior styling, situation and broader social significance within the community. A few representative structures have been selected for careful scrutiny in this category. Second, the dwellings of Calgary's working-class population will be considered. Although these buildings cannot be thought of as monuments of domestic architecture, they are nevertheless important statements of certain attitudes, preferences, and, above all, economic realities which shaped the lives of Calgary workingmen and their families. Third, and in conjunction with working-class housing, the rise in popularity of apartment buildings will be outlined. Whereas apartments were initially the privilege of the middle and upper classes, they became a common form of accommodation for workers after 1912 when immigration to the city reached a peak, and despite some opposition to them by city officials.

# Residences of the Entrepreneurial and Managerial Classes

As noted, the expansion of railway lines across the western plains injected new vitality into the city of Calgary. A wildly growing market for goods and services opened new doors for local entrepreneurs; wholesaling, retailing, manufacturing, construciton and real estate speculation consequently flourished. The upshot of this prairie boom was that the city experienced an era of unprecedented prosperity prior to World War I. While the effects of this new-found opulence were spread across the entire city, the bulk was concentrated in the hands of a few individuals.[1] Entrepreneurs such as William Roper Hull, A.E. Cross, James Lougheed, Pat Burns, T.J.S. Skinner, W.H. Cushing and James Walker benefitted greatly on account of their early arrival and their unceasing toil in establishing successful business ventures in Calgary. Others including Fred C. Lowes, Alex and H.N. Sereth, E.H. Crandell, William Tregillus, O.S. Chapin, John Hextall and R.B. Bennett were relative latecomers to the city, but were able to rise in prominence as well during the boom years through sheer aggressiveness, business acumen and good fortune.[2] Together, these men constituted a dynamic élite. Their wealth, political prowess and social influence were manifest throughout the city in diverse real estate holdings, commercial and industrial undertakings as well as the personal indulgence of their life styles.

The most extravagant expression of the ascendancy of this group was in their homes. Generally speaking, Calgary's men of means had risen quickly from humbler ranks; the novelty of their wealth and achievement thus shone through intensely in the confident, flamboyant spirit of their domestic architecture. So, too, did their ardent desire for public recognition.[3] The construction of pretentious, romantically styled mansions which called forth the admiration of each passerby fulfilled this need. Moreover, careful craftsmanship, rich decoration both inside and out, and aesthetic location on verdant grounds suggested a level of luxury and comfort beyond the means of most people.

Another notable characteristic of these houses was their architectural boldness. Rugged, massive qualities symbolized the power and affluence of Calgary's *nouveaux riches*. This effect, achieved largely through the use of local sandstone, brick and half-timbered motifs, lent an air of solidity to the urban residential environment. As well as providing a traditional, rooted setting where new generations of society's leaders could be nurtured, these lavish homes earned the city an excellent reputation elsewhere. *Construction*, a professional journal published in Toronto for architects and builders in Canada, reported to a national audience that Calgary mansions were clear evidence of the permanent nature of the centre's prosperity and the abiding faith of its citizens in continued progress.

> *In residence architecture, we are safe in saying that Calgary has more high-class, elaborate and expensive homes than any city between Winnipeg and the coast. This indicates two things; first, that there is much wealth in Calgary, and second, that the importance of the city as a centre has attracted to it some very able architects.*[4]

Calgary's prestigious dwellings aptly expressed the thriving conditions of the age. Many were built before 1905, however, signalling the early dominance of the entrepreneurial and managerial classes.[5] William Pearce's lofty estate, for example, was built in 1889 and remained one of the finest structures in the region for years.[6] Another picturesque residence was that erected for Senator James Lougheed in 1892, and nobly referred to as Beaulieu. One of the grandest sandstone villas in the city, it was asymmetrical in plan and essentially Italianate in massing, with heavy, rock-faced masonry walls, round-arched windows and classical detailing throughout.[7] Inside, the decor was equally impressive: Italian marble, Spanish mahogany, antique furniture from England and an elaborate use of stained glass presented a setting that was sufficiently dignified for entertaining even members of the royal family.[8] Just a stone's throw away was the mansion of Patrick Burns. Built in 1901 on a design created by architect Francis M. Rattenbury of Victoria,[9] the building was a fine example of the latest in Edwardian domestic styling. Symmetrical, steeply pitched gables, ornate carvings in the sandstone and a wide carriage round at the entrance gave it the appearance of an English country estate. It was a remarkably handsome structure, incontrovertible evidence of the wealth, power and resourcefulness of Burns who, through his own personal ambition, was able to rise from abject poverty to the top of perhaps the greatest financial empire in western Canada. Other impressive dwellings were erected in this early period by D.W. Marsh, A.E. Cross, Peter Prince, L.H. Doll, Thomas Underwood, Dr.T.H. Blow, and W.B. Barwis.

Viewed collectively, these buildings enshrined the achievement of status of Calgary's social and economic leaders, and became notable landmarks in the emerging metropolis.[10]

After 1905, the number of illustrious homes in the city proliferated. The opening of the Mount Royal subdivision by the CPR in this period, as well as Sunalta, Elbow Park, Elboya, Glencoe, and Bowness, coincided with Calgary's most frantic economic development and provided new enclaves for the growing population of capitalists and professionals. The result was that the landscape rapidly became dotted with beautiful and commodious dwellings. In 1912 alone, 243 residences worth over $4,000 each were built in the city.[11] Since it would be impossible to present an exhaustive survey of these structures, a few representative examples will be carefully examined below.

Home of William Roper Hull, Calgary, c. 1911

William Roper Hull's magnificent estate was built in the same year that Alberta became a province. Located in the heart of the city's first exclusive district at the corner of Twelfth Avenue and Sixth Street West, it was an imposing sight. The building was organized on a square plan, and the structural components were sandstone and brick, thereby giving it a massive appearance. It rose in strong relief against its extensive grounds which covered an impressive twenty-two city lots.[12] In front of the main façade, well-kept gardens were embroidered with colourful flowers. To one side, a cluster of young spruce trees artistically arranged along the estate boundary complemented this adornment. In the back, the lawn was meticulously laid out in gently rolling terraces, providing ample space for the enjoyment of outdoor activities.[13] Roper Hull reportedly entertained large crowds at extravagant garden parties and engaged in such leisurely pastimes as lawn-bowling, croquet and tennis.[14]

William Roper Hull was one of the most distinguished leaders of Calgary business and society. Originally a rancher, he made his fortune before 1900 in the meat-packing business.[15] He bought and sold numerous large ranches in southern Alberta,[16] and later concentrated his capital investments in local industry and real estate.[17] Among the buildings he owned in Calgary were the Hull Block, later sold to and renamed after Pat Burns, the Hull Opera House, the Victoria Block, the Alberta Block, the Albion Block and the Grain Exchange Building.[18] The Roper Hull mansion, Langmore as it was called, thus came to symbolize with all its splendid features the achievement and economic potency of its owner.

Designed by Calgary architects Hodgson and Bates,[19] the house cost $12,000 to construct and an additional $3,000 to furnish.[20] It included two full storeys, an attic level and a basement. The walls were brick, presumably load bearing,[21] while sandstone was used as a foundation material and in decorative flourishes—quoins, piers, lintels and voussoirs— which emphasized the quality of strength in the building. Two boldly projecting bays exposed in all storeys of the front façade also enhanced this effect in their tower-like appearance. Both the front and back verandahs were built in two storeys with elegant balustrades, indicating the importance of outdoor life to these members of the leisured class. Other fascinating forms and lines were evident at the roof level and further embellished the ornate character of the house.[22]

William Roper Hull's home was an eclectic composition which combined numerous Classical Revival elements with the traditional character of an English country house. The result was a well proportioned and pleasing structure with a powerful sense of individualism which, interestingly, was very much the vogue in British upper-class circles at the time.[23] The appearance of such a building in Calgary is therefore evidence of the impact of Edwardian metropolitan culture in the far reaches of the Dominion of Canada.

Thomas J.S. Skinner home, Calgary, c. 1911

Like William Roper Hull, Thomas J.S. Skinner came to the Calgary area from England at an early date. Skinner started out as a mail-carrier in the mountains, but took up permanent residence in the frontier community in 1887, at which time he entered the wholesale and realty businesses. Within the space of twenty years he was one of Calgary's most respected businessmen. As well as buying and selling real estate and serving as president of the Alberta Investment Company, by 1912 he was connected with the Western Milling Company, the Standard Soap Company, the Calgary Natural Gas Company, and the Rocky Mountain Development Company.[24] He was also actively involved in the Calgary Board of Trade and the Congress of Chambers of Commerce of the Empire.[25] Skinner's luxurious home, located in the heart of Mount Royal at the corner of Seventh Street and Twenty-second Avenue West, was another expression of the wealth, status and pride of one of the city's most renowned self-made men.

Completed in 1911, the striking residence was organized on a rectangular plan with several projections. An abundance of materials was utilized in the two storeys, attic level and basement, including sandstone, brick, concrete, stucco and brick. The frame was apparently wood; the sandstone masonry on the first one and a half storeys thus merely provided a rugged decorative covering. In the front elevation, two symmetrical gables and a gable dormer with pediment protruded from the roof line. On the ground storey, a generous open verandah skirted the front entrance, shaded by a simple shed roof supported by squared posts and brackets. Above, a small balcony overlooked the portico and grounds.

The Skinner home was to some extent a modern stylized version of an Elizabethan manor. In the upper storeys, the half-timber motif, moulded designs, decorated verges and roof brackets gave it an artful yet rustic appeal. The dark stained timbers presented a particularly interesting contrast in colour and texture to the stone and stucco surfaces, and nostalgically recalled a pre-industrial, pastoral era in English history when vernacular building traditions prevailed. Inside, the Tudor theme was reiterated in wood panelled walls complete with plate rails, wainscotting, ceiling beams and other decorative features.[26] The style of this house was inspired by the Domestic, or Vernacular, Revival Movement which had become influential in Great Britain by the turn of the century.[27] Translated into a twentieth-century context, Skinner's mansion was not only an assertion of social and economic accomplishment, but also evidence of the conscious importation of romantic English imagery into the western Canadian urban scene.

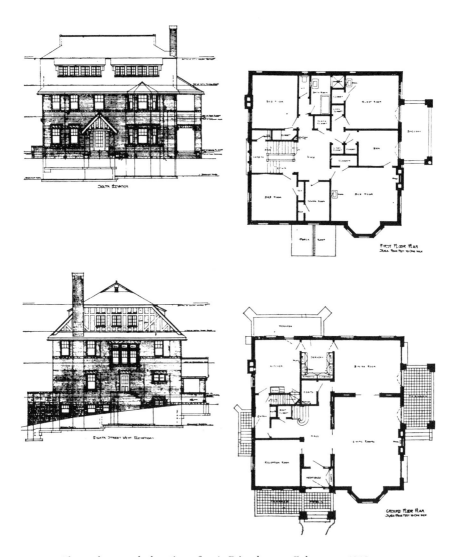

Floor plans and elevations for A. Price home, Calgary, c. 1912

References to English vernacular forms were frequently made in other substantial Calgary homes. In Alfred Price's residence, for example, the simple lines of an old rural building appear to have provided the inspiration for the gambrel type roof, timbered gables and basic square plan. Price was an influential member of the city's managerial class; he came to Calgary in 1907 to assume the position of general superintendent of the CPR for the Alberta Division.[28] His house, suitably located in the CPR subdivision of Mount Royal, was a massive two and a half storey structure designed by architect W.D. Chown.[29] It cost approximately $20,000 to build in 1912,[30] and featured two long, flat dormers in the picturesque roof level, a two-storey bay projecting in the front, and a sizeable verandah and balcony to the side. The facing of the walls was brick veneer, and sandstone was used in the basement as well as the trim. The Price home was charming and homey in external appearance, and fully modern inside. Well-appointed and conveniently laid out rooms presented a highly comfortable environment. Below, the basement served as a garage—a unique feature at that time—with space for four cars. As such, it was an extremely attractive and sophisticated plan, representing, in the words of the *Herald*, "a departure for this city in home design."[31]

Other houses reflected the same bucolic spirit in their styling. On Mount Royal, the residences of Mr. Nunn, A.J. Sayre, L.P. Strong, George Packham,[32] Eugene Coste[33] and others illustrated the increasing popularity of Vernacular Revival features. Meandering streets and huge lots with cheerfully arranged trees and flowers created a tranquil setting that was aesthetically appropriate. Far removed from the smoke of the industrial sector and the humdrum activities of everyday Calgary, these homes provided a sheltered environment that was surrounded by nature and full of tradition, a truly proper sphere for raising a family. Districts along or near the margin of the city's two rivers were especially suited to such splendid domestic architecture. In Bowness, John Hextall implemented some of his plans for an ideal garden suburb in an effort to attract the attention of British capitalists. There, nestled among mature trees, he built several vernacular styled

homes on enormous lots,[34] including his own, together
with an impressive Tudor-styled country club house
overlooking the Bow Valley to the east and the mountains
to the west.[35] These cosy, cottage-like structures had
obvious English antecedents. Although somewhat isolated
from Calgary, they are further evidence of the significance
of imported domestic values in the growing city.

Paralleling the enthusiasm for Vernacular Revival styles was
a certain interest in freer, more open designs, many of
which were of American inspiration or adaptation.[36] Two
and three-storey wood frame houses with characteristically
wide projecting eaves, clapboard or shiplap siding,
decorative shingles and tiles, airy porches, large windows
and commodious rooms offered an elegant, albeit less
formal, atmosphere well suited to the requirements of
family living. At the same time, tasteful embellishments
such as leaded and stained glass, parqueted floors,
wooden shutters and other trim displayed the affluence of
their owners. The stylistic inspirations for these homes
were varied: some were based on the open design of the
Swiss Chalet, while others were derivatives of the California
Bungalow style. Other forms imported from the west coast
were reminiscent of oriental buildings with their bell-cast
roof lines. Rather than simply mimicking specific historical
styles, they were functional, informal family dwellings,
erected in response to the heightened demand for high-
quality homes during the boom period. The predominant
use of wood in these homes can perhaps be attributed to
the abundance of lumber and excellent craftsmen in the
city, and conversely, to inconsistent supplies of brick and
stone at the peak of the boom.

Regardless of the particular forms and styles adopted in
the homes of Calgary's more prosperous inhabitants, a
number of observations can be made on the significance of
these buildings. First of all, it is clear that the function of
these homes went far beyond providing mere physical
shelter. Calgary's most opulent mansions were highly
visible symbols of achievement which publicized the
wealth and power of their owners who, while not an
aristocracy in the sense of inherited privilege, were set
apart from the rest of society by their obvious material

affluence. The homes of the ascendant classes also exhibited great experimentation in styles, materials, comforts and services, indicating that their owners were patrons of superior taste in art and architecture, the vanguard of twentieth century urban culture in Calgary. Finally, these residences reflect a conception of the home as a unique social institution. Members of the entrepreneurial and managerial classes generally viewed the home as a special environment where love of beauty could be cultivated, either through gardening, art, or other activities; where guests could be formally entertained; where leisurely activities could be freely pursued and enjoyed; and most of all, where families could be raised, and where élitist values, traditions and attitudes could be instilled into future generations.[37]

# Residences of the Working Class

During the period that the building boom was in full swing, working-class dwellings became by far the most visible element in the urban landscape. While some structures were truly unique in design, most were built from common plans, mass-produced to meet the ravenous demands of the population explosion. In contrast to the palatial residences of Calgary's affluent citizens, these buildings were humble, utilitarian, yet adequate for workers and their families. Taking into consideration the critical housing shortage from 1905 to 1909, and the fact that a great many newcomers to the city had never before owned their own homes, these simple residences must have seemed lavish. At this time, various important members of society supported the workers in their need for accommodation, arguing from a Smilesean point of view that a contented work force would be more productive, would be better citizens and would enhance the city's reputation as an economic and social leader.[38]

Prior to the boom years, housing for working-class people was difficult to find. Serious shortages were noted as early as 1905.[39] In 1906, the *Herald* reported that few house agents could supply one-tenth of the demand for modern dwellings on account of population increases.[40] Vacancy rates were generally very low between 1905 and 1909 owing to stringent financial conditions, and many people opted to live in tents rather than pay exorbitant rents or real estate prices.[41] Since there had never been a period of oversupply in housing in the city's history, newly-arrived settlers had to rely heavily on whatever residences were built from year to year, with the result that there was intense competition for better quality dwellings.

To complicate matters for workingmen, the insatiable demand for houses led to an overall increase in rents. In 1906, it cost between $30 and $35 a month to rent a modern six to eight-room house, as compared to $25 or lower for a similar house a year earlier.[42] In 1907, rents climbed to between $35 and $45 a month,[43] and by 1909 it cost as much as $50 a month to lease a house.[44] Relentless population pressure inflamed the situation further.

Relief came, however, in 1909 when building activity began to pick up. Spiralling rents stimulated the construction of both owner-occupied houses and rental income properties for investors. But the principal factors which accelerated building construction were the availability of loan and mortgage money at reasonable interest rates and the abundance of relatively inexpensive residential lots in new subdivisions. Money could be borrowed at as low a rate as 5 percent,[45] while lots in outlying districts could be obtained for as little as $75.[46] Easy terms of purchase and payment offered by builders and realtors made it financially viable for many workers to own rather than rent their accommodation.[47] "Don't pay rent," urged an advertisement in the *Albertan*, "when $150 down and $15 per month will pay for a nice cottage and lot."[48] Real estate companies often required one-quarter or less of the full price as down payment on a house, with the balance paid monthly.[49] Similar arrangements were also made for the acquisition of residential land.

With the sudden change in economic circumstances, housing construction rapidly took off. Dwellings constituted over 75 percent of the total number of buildings erected in the boom period and, not surprisingly, the overwhelming majority of these houses were for workers and their families. In 1912, for example, out of a total of 2,416 residences built, 2,173 cost $4,000 or less.[50] Clearly the largest market for houses was the working-class population of the city. To a great extent, realtors and developers catered to their needs by trying to keep homes within the range of their incomes. The market for lower to middle-class housing was subsequently deluged by countless lots in newly-opened districts across the city, and fortunately higher prices were held off for a time. Relatively affordable housing also continued because of the fact that local carpenters often built dwellings from common plans, and the fact that many home-owners were able to assemble their own prefabricated house packages.

## Building Permits for Residences, 1909-1913

| Year | Total Permits | Permits for Residences |
|------|---------------|------------------------|
| 1909 | 777 | 617 |
| 1910 | 1,499 | 1,160 |
| 1911 | 2,619 | 2,054 |
| 1912 | 3,483 | 2,416 |
| 1913 | 2,078 | 1,500 (estimated) |
| Total: | 10,456 | 7,747 |

Sources:  *Calgary Daily Herald*, January 4, 1910; *The Morning Albertan*, February 28, 1911; January 4, 1912; *Henderson's Calgary Directory*, 1913.

The importance of providing workers with adequate accommodation was well known in Calgary at this time. Workers' housing was a crucial issue across Canada, and the *Herald* was quick to point out its serious implications for the national economy.

*All men are influenced by their environment.*
*There isn't any question about it. If the workmen*
*employed in the factories live in unsanitary*
*districts their efficiency must necessarily be*
*impaired . . . No manufacturer who therefore is*
*worthy of the name is satisfied with inefficient*
*workmen any more than he is with inefficient*
*machines.*[51]

The *Herald* added that because there was a deficiency in
skilled labour in the country, manufacturers had a unique
obligation to help establish sanitary and attractive housing
in order to draw workers to industrial centres.[52] In
response to this situation, officials of the CPR announced
that half a section of land adjoining the enormous Ogden
shops would be subdivided and reserved at low prices for
employees who wished to build homes.[53] As well as
demonstrating a sense of corporate responsibility, the CPR
also intended to build up a substantial and reliable supply
of labour near its operations. City officials, too, realized the
importance of the new subdivisions, and thus took steps
quickly to ensure that utilities and services—water and
sewer lines, electric power and the street railway—were
available in these new districts.

Broadly speaking the ownership of private property was
seen as a good thing; workingmen could learn to be thrifty,
independent and diligent by owning their own homes,
thus ensuring social stability. With respect to working-class
housing, W.R. Trotter observed in an address to the Trades
and Labour Council at Calgary in 1911 that satisfaction of
the "home instinct" would also strengthen the bonds of
citizenship among the people.

*What degree of comfort and happiness is*
*experienced by the masses of people must be*
*largely if not altogether determined by their*
*social environment, and one may expect to find a*
*greater loyalty to the national ideal where these*
*factors are in accord with the will of the people*
*and determined by them than will be found . . .*
*where autocratic, bureaucratic or aristocratic*
*[influences control] the governing body.*[54]

The moral support given to workers was certainly helpful, but more important in opening the door to the construction of inexpensive housing was the sudden change of economic conditions in 1909. In contrast to the stately mansions of the civic élite, the working-class dwellings erected during this period were pragmatic solutions to fundamental physical and emotional needs. Some designs provided more than just minimal comforts, but by and large most were simply "good, ordinary houses which served as real homes."[55] Architectural flourishes were typically absent; simplicity of design and honesty of craftsmanship were more in keeping with the informal life style of working-class people. Of primary concern to workers was accommodation that was economical— houses which met family needs for shelter, privacy and friendship, but were worth the cost. Proximity to place of employment was also highly desirable, and districts such as East Calgary, Eau Claire, Bridgeland and Riverside were especially popular in the early years. After 1909, however, the operation of the electric street railway gave workers greater mobility. Suburbs very quickly stretched northward beyond Hillhurst and Crescent Heights to Balmoral and Rosedale, westward beyond Sunalta and Knob Hill to Rosscarrock and Parkdale, southward to Ogden and Ceepeear, and eastward to Fairview and Albert Park.

Workers and their families had numerous house designs from which to choose during these years of frantic construction. The British Columbia Mills, Timber and Trading Company, western Canada's largest lumber establishment, produced a variety of prefabricated house packages in their factories on the Pacific coast.[56] Of these, plans from the Settlers' Series and the Town House Series proved to be the most popular across the prairies. Prices varied markedly: "Design A," a simple one room "sawed hut," 12 feet square, cost $100 while "Design K," a small cottage of three rooms which featured a roof dormer and bay window and measured 20 feet by 25 feet 6 inches, cost $350[57]. "Design M-M," a deluxe version which cost $675, had three comfortable bedrooms in its two storeys but required a lot larger than the normal 25 feet to accommodate its dimensions of 24 feet by 33 feet 6 inches. The advantages

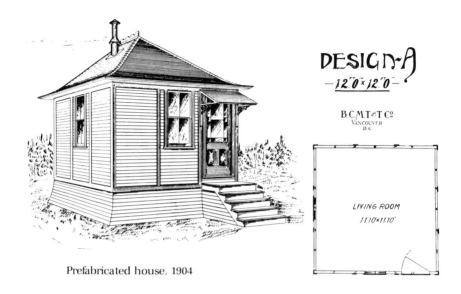

DESIGN·A

−12′0″×12′0″−

B.C.M.T.&T.Co.
Vancouver
B C

LIVING ROOM
11.10″×11.10′

Prefabricated house, 1904

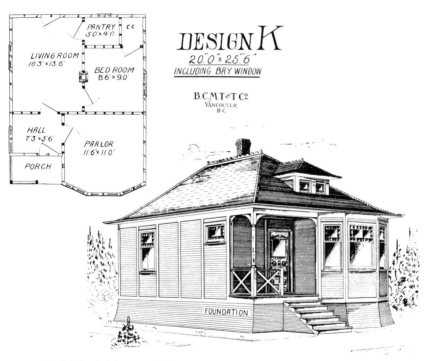

PANTRY
5.0″×9.0′

LIVING ROOM
10.3′×13.6′

BED ROOM
8.6′×9.0′

HALL
7.3′×5.6′

PARLOR
11.6′×11.0′

PORCH

DESIGN K

20′0″×25′6″
INCLUDING BAY WINDOW

B.C.M.T.&T.Co.
Vancouver
B C

FOUNDATION

Prefabricated house, 1904

of these homes were well advertised. Each structure was pre-assembled, numbered on the inside and painted on the outside prior to shipment. An itemized list of materials and an illustrated plan provided clear directions so that "anyone having an ordinary knowledge of tools"[58] could erect one without difficulty. The Company stated in writing that "two men should be able to enclose these buildings from one to four days, according to the size of the plan adopted,"[59] thus saving a considerable amount of money for the workingman. A further advantage was their pleasing, home-like appearance. The visual attractiveness of the Company's products was stressed in an effort to dispel rumours about their general quality, and to gain a foothold in the local house market alongside homes built by carpenters.

Architectural drawing and sketch of bungalow, 1904

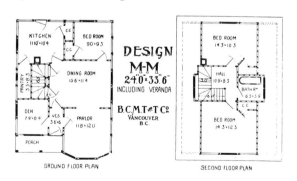

Prudential Builders Limited was another company which was geared to the mass production of inexpensive housing. Like the British Columbia Mills, it had its own lumber mill and manufacturing complex where pre-cut house components were made.[60] One plan, the "Calgary" model, was specifically suited to local climatic conditions and was successfully marketed during the city's boom period.[61] It featured seven rooms on two levels, including four bedrooms, kitchen, living and dining rooms, a bathroom, pantry, alcove and a verandah running across the front.[62] Most probably other major lumber plants, such as the Crown Lumber Company which was linked to large industrial facilities and an extensive distributing network, also engaged in the marketing of similar sectional homes.[63]

In addition to the erection of ready-made structures, much copy building went on in Calgary. One syndicate, the Canadian Home Investment Company, built houses on a large scale across the city from at least five plans.[64] Another organization which arranged for the construction, financing and sale of dwellings was the Home Loan and Contract Company. Backed by English capital, Home Loan built many $1,200 bungalows from a basic plan[65]. Local

Row of houses in Calgary, c. 1912-1914

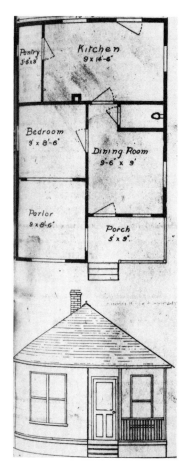

Floor plan and front elevation
of small bungalow, Calgary, 1912

carpenters were employed in great numbers by these and other companies, such as Messieurs Robertson and Carlile Limited who erected houses for both rental and purchase speculation.

Individual architects and builders in the city were also kept busy designing economical homes for the masses. In addition to providing private consultation, Holman and Gotch,[66] William Emery,[67] and Henderson and Brown[68] designed many plans which appeared in the *Herald* in 1912 advertising the value of professional advice for home buyers. In many cases, the plans were of sufficient detail that small-scale contractors could easily copy or adapt them to their own construction work within the city. The *Herald* also encouraged readers to erect their own homes from plans published each week, and carried articles on topics ranging from interior decorating to sanitation and gardening. Beginning in March 1912, nearly every Monday edition featured a page which was devoted to promoting awareness and interest in current domestic fashions. Many of the ideas presented therein to its readers were developed and tested in the cities of the United States. The bungalow style, for example, much publicized by local designers Holman and Gotch and Emery, was a product of the California environment. Its adoption in Calgary is ample illustration of the commonality of urban growth in North America and the impact of American ingenuity on architectural tastes in western Canada.

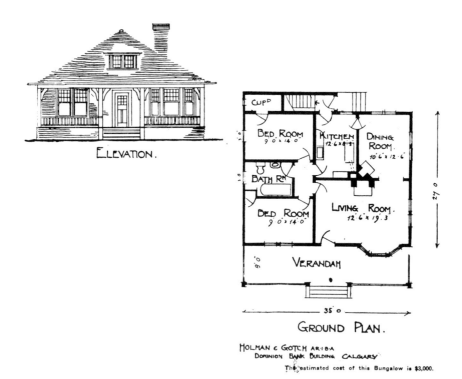

Ground plan and elevation drawing of bungalow, Calgary, 1912

# To Own His Home---How and Where To Build---Suggestions for Plans.

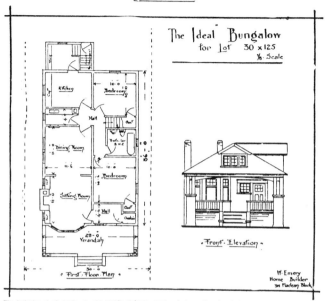

The Ideal Bungalow
for Lot 30 x 125
⅛ Scale

- Front - Elevation -

W. Emery
Home Builder
301 Maclean Block

- First - Floor - Plan -

The designing of a bungalow for this size lot at a moderate cost requires a little practical, as well as architectural knowledge. There is always a danger of sacrificing light and internal convenience for external effect.

This bungalow is designed from a general knowledge of the requirements needed in Calgary.

Some of this bungalow's leading features are, a small entrance hall with closet provided for cloaks, leading to sitting room, with bay windows, and open fireplace, dining room with small stairway pantry, bedroom between kitchen; a covered entrance to back and basement entrance. There is also complete privacy given to bathroom, and sleeping accommodation.

The pitch of roof allows for two bedrooms to be constructed in same, making four bedrooms, or three bedrooms and good sized box room.

The following specifications are carried out in the construction, which can be altered to suit requirements: Full basement, 9 inch concrete walls, beam fitted, concrete basement floor, 2x4 inch framing, 1x8 inch ship la boarding to outside walls; good stron building paper and shingles to ro and sides.

First floor, 2x8 incr joists, commo boards and edge grained flooring finished floor, fir finish throughout, ir cluding fir doors. All woodwork stair ed and varnished to approved stain flat finish if required. Walls ced smooth finish prepared for kalsomit or paper. Plumbing work fully mo ern throughout. The approximate co of this bungalow complete is $2,500.

Floor plan and front elevation for bungalow, Calgary, 1912

Bungalow designs were particularly appealing to Calgary's working-class population. Inspired to a large degree by the Craftsman Movement in the United States, particularly the work of Los Angeles architects Greene and Greene, and colonial residences in India,[69] the bungalow was a practical, gracious frame structure which could be erected at a relatively low cost. Simplicity of design and finish were the keynotes of the style.[70] All pretensions and extravagant effects, either inside or out, were to be avoided, since they were not in keeping with the bungalow spirit. Ideally, a bungalow consisted of "no more than an absolutely necessary number of rooms,"[71] plus an attic or small second storey. It was further characterized by simple, horizontal lines, a wide projecting roof, numerous large windows and woodwork of the plainest kind.[72] Comfort and integrity were emphasized throughout, rather than ostentation and luxury. The bungalow was not designed as a status symbol, but to create and contain a congenial atmosphere conducive to harmonious family relations and relaxed living. Its beauty lay in its utility, its versatility and, above all, its humble charm.[73]

Other house styles were prominent in working-class districts, but apart from external differences, all dwellings served a basic purpose of meeting the physical, emotional and social needs of the city's lower income population. They also offered privacy for workers' families and refuge from an increasingly complex society wherein peace of mind could be restored. Moreover, the quality of life they offered to their occupants was generally respectable. Compared with the crowded tenement dwellings in British and eastern North American centres, these homes must have seemed spacious and well-built.[74] Floor plans ranging from 650 to 750 square feet were not uncommon for two bedroom bungalows situated on small 25 to 30 foot wide lots in subdivisions near Calgary's main industrial areas. In more remote districts such as Killarney, Altadore, Crescent Heights and North Balmoral, where land was typically cheaper, houses were often even larger.[75]

With regard to utilities and services in Calgary, indoor plumbing and water were apparently available in a substantial proportion of the homes erected during the boom years. In 1909, 971 water closets, 896 sinks and 592 baths were installed, whereas only 617 permits were taken out for residence construction.[76] By 1912, the discrepancy between the number of service connections made and the number of housing starts was even more noticeable. That year, 4,811 water closets, 3,862 sinks and 3,181 baths were installed, compared to 2,416 building permits for residences.[77] Successive extensions of water and sewer lines and reasonably low prices for service to customers made it possible for most property owners to benefit from these amenities.[78] Underlying this was the fundamental concern of city administrators to create and control an advanced physical environment for a rapidly growing population, and thereby protect the local citizens from the threat of communicable disease.[79] Electrical power was also relatively inexpensive during this period, after May 1911 when Calgary Power Limited began operation of its new Horseshoe Falls plant on the Kananaskis River.[80]

Similarly, with the completion of the Canadian Western Natural Gas, Light, Heat and Power Company's pipeline from Bow Island to Calgary in 1912, gas became available to local consumers at the low price of thirty-five cents per thousand cubic feet.[81] Prior to the arrival of the natural gas pipeline, coal and artificially produced coal gas had been widely used for fuel in workers' homes.[82] However, because of the advantages of natural gas in cheapness, abundance of supply and cleanness of combustion, these other domestic energy sources were quickly displaced, By September 30, 1912, there were 2,500 gas services in operation in the city; two years later Canadian Western had a total of 12,000 customers in Alberta, most of whom were Calgary residents.[83]

Altogether then, Calgary workingmen and their families enjoyed a level of comfort and convenience in their new homes that was unsurpassed in many cities elsewhere. With the dramatic change in the financial climate in 1909, the dream of home ownership suddenly became a reality for many, thus enhancing the pride and contentment of the local working class.[84] Furthermore, the grouping of these homes in new, distinctively lower income subdivisions helped to foster a sense of community among the workers, and as well an awareness that they too had a common stake in the city's future.

# Apartments and High-Density Structures

Residential patterns of Calgary's burgeoning population between 1905 and 1915 indicate that the detached single-family dwelling was by far the most strongly preferred form of housing. Workingmen from crowded urban centres in Great Britain and eastern Canada despaired of high-density living, and therefore shunned the images of "living factories" upon coming to the west. They saw great opportunity for self-advancement in the new country. The prospect of owning a home, in particular, filled most with a hope of attaining greater economic freedom and social respectability. Yet with continued population pressure, escalating real estate values and stricter economic conditions in 1913, fewer workers were able to attain this goal. Rental accommodation once again became scarce because of intensified demand. As a result, apartment construction accelerated between 1911 and 1913, and the lower income people in the city were compelled to accept high-density dwellings as a solution to their housing needs.

Prior to the crest of the boom, apartments in Calgary were largely the domain of certain members of the affluent classes. While most entrepreneurs and professional people were inclined to live in respectable private homes, others who had left their families behind, were single or had travelled a great deal consequently found that apartment life had definite advantages. Apartments offered a comfortable and modern environment often located near the city's central business district. Furthermore, they freed their tenants from the domestic responsibilities imposed by home ownership, thus allowing them more time to socialize with their associates and clients.

Rental prices were high, however, and prohibited all but the well-to-do from enjoying these conveniences. At the Marlborough Mansions, for example, a suite could be rented for $45 a month in December 1908,[85] compared to $35 a month for an average size house in a good locality.[86]

In spite of the cost, growing numbers of local inhabitants were attracted by the virtues of apartment living. At the same time, city officials evidently supported the development of higher quality apartment buildings as they tended to attract tenants from the upper classes, which further enhanced the character of Calgary's prestigious districts. With this demand for premium rental accommodation, then, numerous luxurious structures were erected. Of these, few were as striking as the Devenish Apartment Building on Seventeenth Avenue and Eighth Street West. Designed by Alex Pirie, it was built on a rectangular plan one city block long and three storeys in height. Crenelated turrets at each corner and decorative parapets in the front façade gave it the appearance of an enormous castle, while the entrances were accented with classical details. The building was constructed of solid brick[87] on a concrete foundation, and was ornamented with sandstone trim around the windows. Fifty-seven spacious suites and numerous special features provided a maximum of comfort to residents, among whom were some of the community's most illustrious members (see Appendix A for information on occupancy).

Devenish apartment building, Calgary, 1913

The Connaught Apartment Building, located on the corner of Fourth Avenue and Sixth Street West, was perhaps the most extravagant edifice of its kind in the city. A three-storey solid brick structure composed of twelve large and luxuriously appointed suites,[88] it was designed by J.J. O'Gara and opened for public inspection in January 1913.[89] The building was remarkably handsome. Situated on splendid grounds directly across from the picturesque Calgary Normal School, it was elegantly symmetrical, and finished throughout in solid birch mahogany, clear maple flooring, and artistically hung wallpaper.[90] It also offered the most up-to-date domestic conveniences, including a built-in Tuec vacuum cleaner system with outlets in every suite, a garbage incinerator and a Kribble Vapor Vacuum heating system, one of the most successful steam units on the market[91] (see Appendix A).

Other higher class apartment houses were similarly located close to the city's business centre. The area skirting Central Park near the glamorous residences of the élite became a favoured district for two and three-storey multiple dwellings. Among the many situated there were the Moxam Apartments and Houlton House, next to the Lougheed mansion; Dufferin Lodge, across from First Baptist Church; the Lorraine Apartments, across from Pat Burns's and William Roper Hull's estates; the Crandell and Hester Apartment Buildings and the Hermitage.[92]

With the sudden flood of immigrants into the city during the peak years of 1912 and 1913, the occupancy structure of apartments in Calgary changed drastically. The steady influx of a thousand people a month kept the demand for apartments and houses considerably in excess of the supply. Rental prices consequently continued to rise.[93] Real estate values also climbed sharply, more than doubling in price in some working-class districts,[94] and thereby limited the number of people who could afford to buy homes. As a result, the construction of rental property—both single-family and multiple-family dwellings—took off at an astronomical rate as investors found a rewarding opportunity for high returns on their money. Whereas in 1911 there had been twenty-five apartments in the city,[95] by 1913, eighty-one were listed in the *Tregillus-Thompson Directory* for Calgary.[96] Many of the structures erected were clearly intended to meet the needs imposed by the swollen working-class population. Changed conditions in the local labour market contributed to workers' rapid acceptance of high-density living. In spite of an oversupply in many of the trades in Calgary, demographic pressure was relentless in 1913. And with the sudden scarcity of finance capital in the city, construction slowed to a virtual standstill, causing wide-spread unemployment in the building industry.[97] For those workers who were fortunate enough to have steady jobs in other sectors of the local economy, the options for accommodation were somewhat restricted; but for others who found themselves being pushed closer to the brink of poverty, the alternatives were few indeed.

While the high density dwellings represented a more efficient use of urban land and offered a superficially attractive solution to the problem of accommodation for the growing population of the working class, top City of Calgary officials generally perceived apartments in negative terms. Building Inspector H.A. Sylvester described them as "no more than a necessary evil at best" and ". . . a menace."[98] It was believed that the erection of apartment buildings tended to hurt surrounding neighbourhoods due to the gradual delapidation and neglect of rental units by tenants, and the subsequent decline in the class of occupants.[99]

Slums, the bugbear of older eastern centres, were to be avoided in Calgary where, according to Sylvester, the opportunity for rightly ordered development still existed.[100] Furthermore, it was thought that apartments were "a municipal parasite" in that tenants shared all the advantages of public utilities and civic amenities but bore only a small percentage of the burden of local property tax.[101] Restrictions for apartment buildings were consequently made quite rigid in Calgary. For example, the city's new Building Ordinance By-law which was passed in 1912 required that no less than two-thirds of the owners of land in a block where an apartment was proposed give their approval for its construction.[102] However, while the task of regulating indiscriminate apartment construction was commendable, the Building Department was still compelled to deal with the reality of accommodation shortages and to permit selective development of poorer quality structures on that basis.

Of the multitude of apartments and tenement dwellings built for the working-class population between 1911 and 1913, a substantial number were located in East Calgary, close to the city's industrial districts. These included the Befus, Burn, Carson and Dougall Blocks on Ninth Avenue East, and the Hillier and Samis Blocks, Sevenoaks Court and the Louise Apartments immediately east of the downtown area. Some were also erected in Broadview near the car-line, including the Phyllis Apartments, the Florence Apartments, and the Gordon, Kerr, Ross and Vendome Blocks. Others yet, such as the Morasch Apartments, the Poffenroth Apartments and the Isabella Block were to be found elsewhere, scattered in the city's principal working-class districts of Bridgeland, Crescent Heights and Bankview (see Appendix A).

The vast majority of these structures were cheaply constructed and austere in appearance. Red pressed brick manufactured locally[103] or at Redcliffe, Alberta, was commonly used as a veneer over either a wooden or reinforced concrete frame. Essentially classical in their simple, severe forms, most had little more than a pressed metal cornice and sandstone trim for ornamentation. Economy of materials and plainness of design were stressed. Many also had retail space in the ground level in order to make them better paying investments for their owners.[104] Inside, most of these structures offered often crowded and rough living quarters to tenants, conditions that were definitely a step below that available in most single family residences in workers' districts. These buildings therefore stood in striking contrast to the opulent and imposing apartment dwellings of the professional, managerial and entrepreneurial classes. As well, they represented a reluctant departure from the preferred norm of single-family dwellings for the working-class population in the city.

*     *     *

In the residential landscape which emerged between 1905 and 1915, the reality of both an aggressive entrepreneurial and managerial elite and a substantial working-class population were strikingly apparent. Extravagant mansions openly declared the indomitable spirit of Calgary's commercial and corporate leaders, while street after street of simple, mass-built bungalows and cottages revealed the presence of the ubiquitous labour force. Toward the beginning of the war, apartment buildings and tenement dwellings began to appear in large numbers as well, signalling tightened economic conditions and spiralling land values across the city. Also evident was the impact of modern, twentieth-century metropolitan culture in the form of various house styles, design features, domestic conveniences and amenities, building materials and construction techniques. Ostentatious residences, with their ornamental flourishes in masonry, glass and woodwork, provided a suitable display for the recently acquired wealth and status of their owners. In addition, the availability of cheap, high-quality lumber and industrially-manufactured sectional houses from the west coast, inexpensive pressed brick, cement and other locally produced materials enabled many Calgarians to erect their own homes.

Despite a serious housing shortage in the first half of the decade, the population of the city swelled as opportunities for the successful employment of capital and labour expanded wildly. The availability of substantial money for mortgages and loans after 1908 caused local construction, particularly house construction, to accelerate. But increased immigration to the city during 1912 and 1913, and then the collapse of the boom in 1913 changed the housing situation drastically, especially for the working-class population. Many workingmen were forced to abandon their hope of owning a home, and to take up residence in high-density dwellings similar to the structures they had lived in before coming to the west.

Henry Vivian, a British planning expert and Member of Parliament who visited the city, found good reason to stand against the trend toward tenement living in Canada. In an address to some of Calgary's more prominent citizens, he offered cogent advice clothed in imperialistic rhetoric.

*. . . We in our cities should not, Mr. Mayor,
accept the principle of tenement dwelling for the
ideal home . . . You are not able to see the effect
of existing home life on efficiency merely in one
generation. I have seen in London, during my
twenty-five years of very close contact with
London life—more particularly among the
working classes—. . . that the effect of tenement
dwelling upon efficiency is very bad indeed . . .
The full effect falls on the wife, and later on the
children, and if you take three generations, then
you have got the full effect. . . The British race,
what has made it so strong as it is in the world is
the strong individuality of character. . . I believe,
Mr. Mayor, the future of our Empire and the
future of our race depends upon our
preservation of those conditions that make for
the retention and strength of that individuality. . .
The individual home, the individual family, the
individual brought up in the home, and the
association of home life—upon that all our
success depends.*[105]

City officials and the leaders of the city planning
movement thus offered sound reasons why high density
living conditions were undesirable in Calgary, but as in
other prairie centres the forces of the regional economy
proved more potent in shaping residential patterns. The
construction of single family dwellings for the working-
class consequently slowed as western Canada entered a
time of recession. Continued immigration into the
community from less buoyant regions and countries,
increased unemployment and rapidly dwindling sources
of finance capital further weakened Calgary's social and
economic situation. Housing once again became scarce
and expensive; the land of opportunity thus proved to be
a land of disappointment for many, particularly those who
perilously ventured forth in the advent of economic
recession and war.

# Notes

[1]See Paul Voisey, "In Search of Wealth and Status," in *Frontier Calgary*, ed. Rasporich and Klassen, pp. 221-241.

[2]See A.O. MacRae, *History of the Province of Alberta*, 2 vols. (Calgary: The Western Canada History Company, 1912); also John Blue, *Alberta Past and Present*, 3 vols. (Chicago: Pioneer Historical Publishing Company, 1924), for extensive biographical information on these and other men.

[3]Paul Voisey, "In Search of Wealth and Status," in *Frontier Calgary*, ed. Rasporich and Klassen, pp. 236-237.

[4]*Construction* 3, no. 2 (December 1909): 111. See also James A. Cockburn, *Calgary, Alberta: The City of the Foothills in the Land of the Chinook with its Commercial Houses, Churches, Residences, etc.— Portrayed* (n.p.: n.pub., 1905).

[5]See *Picturesque Calgary* (Calgary: Calgary Herald Publishing Company, 1905) for a more complete view of some of the city's notable residences which were erected in an earlier time.

[6]William Pearce was a Superintendent for Lands and Mines for the Dominion Government and later worked for the CPR's Department of Natural Resources. His home featured a total of fifteen rooms and included such modern comforts as indoor plumbing and running water, steam heat, natural gas, a large refrigerator, a wine cellar, an irrigated garden, three fireplaces, a billiard room and servants' quarters. See Paul Voisey, "In Search of Wealth and Status," p. 238.

[7]See City of Calgary, PHSE, vol. 4, category 15, file 220.

[8]*Herald*, March 8, 1958; Lougheed entertained such royal visitors as the Duke and Duchess of Connaught, Princess Patricia, and the Prince of Wales.

[9]For pictures of the Pearce, Lougheed, Burns and other early sandstone mansions, see Vicky Williams, *Calgary Then and Now* (Vancouver: Bodima Books, 1978) and A.A. Barrett and R.W. Liscombe, *Francis Rattenbury and British Columbia: Architecture and Challenge In the Imperial Age* (Vancouver: University of British Columbia Press, 1983).

[10]See Trudy Soby, *Be It Ever So Humble* (Calgary: Century Calgary Publications, 1975) for pictures of many of these structures.

[11]This figure represents about 10 percent of the total number of residences built in 1912, approximately 20 percent of the total erected in 1910 and 52 percent of the number built in 1909: See *Herald*, June 26, 1909; *Albertan* February 28, 1911 and *Henderson's Calgary Directory*, 1913, p. 147.

[12]MacRae, *History of the Province of Alberta*, vol. 1, p. 583.

[13]See GAI, Photo Archives for other views of the Roper Hull estate.

[14]Voisey, "In Search of Wealth and Status," in *Frontier Calgary*, ed. Rasporich and Klassen, pp. 236-238.

[15]MacRae, *History of the Province of Alberta*, vol. 1, p. 582.

[16]*Ibid.*, pp. 581-583.

[17]*Ibid.*

[18]*News Telegram*, January 11, 1913.

[19]*Construction* 3, no. 2 (December 1909), photograph.

[20]MacRae, *History of the Province of Alberta*, vol. 1, p. 583.

[21]Examination of the structure is impossible as it was demolished in 1970 to make way for a high-rise apartment building.

[22]The use of shaped lapping tiles was reminiscent of pantiles which were common in English vernacular buildings. See R.W. Brunskill, *Illustrated Handbook of Vernacular Architecture* (London: Faber and Faber Limited, 1971; reprint ed., 1978), pp. 92-93.

[23]Alastair Service, *Edwardian Architecture* (London: Oxford University Press, 1977), p. 140. According to Service, Edwardian architects resurrected the classical spirit of England in the Baroque age to commemorate the slowly passing glory of the British Empire prior to World War I.

[24]MacRae, *History of the Province of Alberta*, vol. 1, pp. 514-515.

[25] *Ibid.*

[26] GAI, Photo Archives; these pictures of the Skinner residence were taken in the 1920s, but probably indicate the basic interior finish of the house. The large two-storey tower shown in one of the pictures gave the home the appearance of an Italian villa, but was likely built after the end of the decade studied, as was the impressive greenhouse to the side.

[27] See R.W. Brunskill, *Illustrated Handbook of Vernacular Architecture*, pp. 206-209 for a discussion of the Vernacular Revival in England. See also Service, *Edwardian Architecture*, Chapters Two, Six and Twelve, for a discussion of the domestic revival.

[28] Henry James Morgan, *Canadian Men and Women of the Time* (Toronto: William Briggs, 1912), p. 917.

[29] *Herald*, June 17, 1912.

[30] *Ibid.*

[31] *Ibid.*

[32] *Albertan*, February 28, 1912, "Calgary, the Beautiful City of Homes." See also *Construction* 3, no. 2 (December 1909), for pictures of the residences of Mr. Nunn and A.J. Sayre.

[33] GAI, Photo Archives; photograph of the twenty-eight room Coste house built in 1913.

[34] See *Albertan*, February 28, 1911 for pictures and description of houses being sold in Bowness.

[35] Alberta Culture, Historic Sites Service file on the Bowness Golf Club, Old St. Stephen's College, Edmonton. Vernacular styled buildings were also prevalent in Elboya, Elbow Park and Glencoe.

[36] Plans and pictures of such homes appeared in the *Herald* on April 8 and 29, 1912, for example.

[37] See Mark Girouard, *Life in the English Country House—A Social and Architectural History* (New Haven and London: Yale University Press, 1978), Chapters Ten and Eleven.

[38] Samuel Smiles, British apologist of the work ethic and the Victorian virtues of thrift and self-help, wrote the

following in 1875. "The accumulation of property has the effect which it always has upon thrifty men; it makes them steady, sober and diligent. It weans them from revolutionary notions, and makes them conservative. When working-men, by their industry and frugality, have secured their own independence, they will cease to regard the sight of others' well-being as a wrong inflicted upon themselves; and it will no longer be possible to make political capital out of their imaginary woes." Quoted in David Rubenstein, *Victorian Homes* (London: David and Charles, 1974), pp. 218-219. See also Herbert Ames, *City Below the Hill: A Sociological Study of a Portion of the City of Montreal* (Toronto: University of Toronto Press, 1972) for another Canadian illustration of this viewpoint.

39 *Herald*, October 14, 1905.

40 *Herald*, April 9, 1906.

41 *Herald*, May 3, 1905. Also *Herald*, July 4, 1907. Advertisements for tent structures, such as appeared in the *Albertan* on April 30, 1909, were carried by local newspapers well into the boom period.

42 *Herald*, December 18, 1905, advertisement. Also *Herald*, December 15, 1906, advertisement by W.B. Barwis for an eight-room house, all modern, on Fourteenth Avenue West, to rent at $35 a month.

43 *Herald*, May 2, 1907, advertisement for a small house close to Eighth Avenue, renting at $45 a month; *Herald*, December 3, 1907, advertisement for a seven-room house with a stable at $35 a month.

44 A small, compact, very comfortable house was advertised in the *Herald* on May 1, 1909, for $50 a month. On December 16, 1909, the *Herald* advertised a seven-room, fully modern house at $75 per month, indicating a swift rise in rental prices during the year. Such an increase is remarkable since December was typically a month of slackened demand, and therefore generally lower prices.

45 *Henderson's Directory*, 1912. Among the companies which advertised a 5 percent interest rate on mortgages were the Canadian Home Investment Company (*Herald*, June 13, 1911)

and the North-West Home and Loan Company (*Herald*, May 11, 1912).

[46]Advertisement for lots in Spruce City by Cecil Hadfield; *Albertan*, March 1, 1909.

[47]*Herald*, May 1, 1909.

[48]Advertisement by Bruce Gordon in the *Albertan*, May 12, 1909.

[49]For example, see the *Herald*, July 2, 1909; H.M. Splane and Company offered a six-room cottage for sale in Mills Estate at $1,600, with $400 down and the balance to be paid monthly. Lots in South Calgary were sold at $110 each by Eureka Real Estate Company with similar terms of one-quarter cash and the balance to be paid monthly; see *Herald*, September 28, 1909. On May 13, 1910, C.H. Cruikshank and Company's advertisement in the *Herald* offered houses on even easier terms. For example, a fully modern house on Eighteenth Avenue East worth $3,000 could be purchased with only $400 down.

[50]*Henderson' Directory*, 1913, p. 147.

[51]*Herald*, March 18, 1912.

[52]*Ibid.*

[53]*Herald*, March 23, 1912.

[54]*Souvenir of the Twenty-Seventh Annual Convention of the Trades and Labour Congress of Canada*, Calgary, 1911, Address by W.R. Trotter to the Convention (n.p.: n.pub., 1911).

[55]*Herald*, April 15, 1912.

[56]GAI, *The British Columbia Mills, Timber and Trading Company Catalogue of Patented and Ready-Made Houses* (Vancouver: n.pub., 1905).

[57]*Ibid.*

[58]*Ibid.*

[59]*Ibid.* See also the *Herald*, May 30, 1911; it was common for people to erect their own houses during the boom years.

[60]D.W. Holdsworth and G.E. Mills, "The B.C. Mills Prefabricated System: The Emergence of Ready-Made Buildings in Western Canada," Canadian Historic Sites Occasional Papers in Archaeology and History, no. 14 (Ottawa: Parks Canada, 1975), pp. 149-150.

[61]*Herald*, June 24, 1911, advertisement, p. 14.

[62]*Ibid.*

[63]The Crown Lumber Company Limited was incorporated in 1905. By 1912, fifty-two yards were in operation in different parts of the province. All purchasing was done in Calgary, where warehouses were also maintained from which outside yards were supplied. MacRae, *History of the Province of Alberta*, vol. 1, pp. 566-567. Also, GAI, Crown Lumber Plans and Business Papers.

[64]*Herald*, June 13, 1911, advertisement.

[65]*Herald*, May 6, 1912, p. 21.

[66]*Herald*, April 1, and 22, 1912.

[67]*Herald*, April 15 and May 20, 1912.

[68]*Herald*, August 26 and September 9, 1912.

[69]See Gustav Stickley, *Craftsman Homes — Architecture and Furnishings of the American Arts and Crafts Movement* (New York: Dover Publications, 1979; repr. Craftsman Publishing Company, 1909). Also D. W. Holdsworth, "House and Home in Vancouver: Images of West Coast Urbanism, 1886-1929," in *The Canadian City*, ed. Artibise and Stelter, pp. 195-198. Also W.R. and K. Current, *Greene and Greene — Architects in the Residential Style* (Fort Worth: Amon Carter Museum of Western Art, 1974), pp. 4-5. See also D.W. Holdsworth, "Vernacular Forms in an Urban Context," Chapter One.

[70]*Herald*, April 1, 1912; Stickley, *Craftsman Homes*, pp. 1-5, 194-205.

[71]*Ibid.*

[72]*Ibid.*

[73]See also F.G. Brown, "Bungalow Design and Construction," in *Construction* 1, no. 11 (August 1908); and

"Types of Pacific Coast Homes," 4, no. 3 (January 1911).

[74]The quality of construction of workers' houses was generally satisfactory in Calgary; nevertheless, with large-scale production of inexpensive housing, some jerry-building took place as contractors tried to cut their costs. See *Herald.* September 3, 1912, for contemporary observations on the subject.

[75]Many of the bungalows and cottages described in preceding pages on this chapter were approximately this size.

[76]*Annual Report of the City of Calgary,* 1909. (Calgary: City Clerk, 1910), p. 54.

[77]*Annual Report of the City of Calgary,* 1912 (Calgary: City Clerk, 1913), p. 202.

[78]See GAI City Clerk's Papers, annual reports of civic committees, 1906-1914, and *Annual Reports of the City of Calgary,* 1907-1913, for accounts of the extension and development of local services and utilities. See also the *Herald,* August 4, 1932, for a capsule summary of the Waterworks Department's activities in this period. Despite difficulties in pumping water to outlying districts on the North Hill and South-West Calgary, some problems of supply during winter months and some problems with turbidity, water service was generally good before the war. In 1912, it cost only $5 for a year's supply of water for a five-room house. Quoted from the *Herald* in *Canadian Western Natural Gas: Half a Century of Service 1912-1962* (Calgary: n. pub., 1962).

[79]See *News Telegram,* March 20, 1912, for an example of local health concerns. See also *Annual Reports of the City of Calgary,* 1907-1913, for summary details of civic sanitation and Health Department undertakings.

[80]Power rates dropped significantly because of the abundance of electricity and the fact that the City of Calgary had signed a most generous contract for power supply with the Company, *Some Facts About Calgary Power, Limited,* (Calgary: n.pub., 1962) GAI Calgary Power Papers. "Memorandum of Agreement," September 12, 1910. Also see *Albertan,* May 22, 1911.

[81]Municipal Manual, 1915, p. 67; *Annual Reports of the Canadian Western Natural Gas, Light, Heat and Power Company*, 1912-1915, n.p., n.pub., 1912-1915.

[82]*Ibid.* See *News Telegram*, May 27, 1909, and *Albertan*, October 5, 1911, for details of earlier gas discoveries on Colonel Walker's property in East Calgary, and attempts by A.W. Dingman to service nearby residential subdivisions. While this early work successfully introduced natural gas in the city, it was the technical skill and business daring of Eugene Coste, backed by the Canadian Pacific Railway, that brought it into widespread use in Calgary households. Coste's discovery of a major gas field on CPR land at Bow Island in 1908, and subsequent agreement with Company officials to market the product in Calgary and Lethbridge, furthermore, did much to establish the growing natural gas industry in southern Alberta. See GAI, CPR Papers, "Correspondence between Company officials and Mr. Eugene Coste."

[83]*Annual Reports of Canadian Western Natural Gas Company*, 1912, 1914. Nineteen fourteen was the greatest single year of gas service connections in the city.

[84]This may provide a partial explanation for the stable, conservative character of the Calgary labour movement in the years 1905 to 1912. After 1912, as housing became more scarce and unemployment and inflation became rampant, workers became agitated because of losses in their standard of living. See E.A. Taraska, "The Calgary Craft Union Movement, 1900-1920" (Unpublished Master's thesis, University of Calgary, 1975).

[85]*Herald*, December 22, 1908, advertisement.

[86]*Herald*, December 18, 1908, advertisement by Toole Peet.

[87]*Albertan*, February 28, 1911, p. 31; according to the City of Calgary, PHSE, vol. 1, category 1, file 96, the structure has a reinforced concrete frame within brick exterior bearing walls. On May 1, 1912, the *Herald* listed a furnished suite for rent at $75 per month.

[88]*Herald*, January 4, 1913. Each suite had five rooms: a living room, dining room, kitchen and two bedrooms plus a bathroom and hall. Many also had their own balcony.

[89] *Ibid.*

[90] *Ibid.*

[91] *Tregillus-Thompson Directory,* 1913, pp. 189-190.

[93] In 1909, it cost between $40 and $50 a month to rent an average size house. By 1912, it cost between $55 and $70 to rent similar accommodation. By 1913, over-crowding and high rents became topics which concerned the local press; see *News-Telegram,* February 21, 1913, editorial, and *Albertan,* July 3, 1913, editorial.

[94] Lots in Bridgeland were advertised by William Toole at between $150 and $300 in the *Albertan,* March 24, 1909. On January 2, 1913, the *Herald* carried an advertisement for Bridgeland property by the same agent at $660.

[95] *Henderson's Directory,* 1911.

[96] *Tregillus-Thompson Directory,* 1913.

[97] *Labour Gazette,* vols. 13 and 14, reports of Calgary labour conditions from April to October, 1913. Also, *Calgary Board of Trade Annual Report,* 1913, "Report of the Council," p. 27-28.

[98] See GAI City Clerk's Papers, Box 58, file folder 470.

[99] *Ibid.*

[100] *Ibid.*

[101] *Ibid.*

[102] GAI City of Calgary By-Laws. Building Ordinance #1366, pp. 31-33.

[103] Some of the major brickyards in the city were the Calgary Silicate Pressed Brick Company, Tregillus Clay Products, Crandell Pressed Brick and Sandstone Company, Brick and Supply Limited and the Alberta Pressed Brick Company. As early as 1910, however, the Redcliffe brickyard, advertised in the *Herald* on June 15 as the finest and largest in Canada, began to out-compete local concerns in supplying pressed brick to construction projects.

[104] Among the many buildings which doubled as retail space and rental accommodation were the Ross Block, the

Kerr Block, the Befus Block, the Western Block, the Underwood Building and the Lougheed Building. See *Henderson's Directory*, 1914, for other buildings, along Ninth Avenue South-East, Seventeenth Avenue South-West, and Fourth Street South-West.

[105]Henry Vivian, "How to Apply Town Planning to Calgary," *Construction* 7, no. 1 (November 1913): pp. 385-386.

# 3.

# Schools and Public Buildings

There were fewer than three-quarters of a million people on the Canadian prairies in 1905, but by the time that World War I broke out, almost a million more were added. In the same period, Calgary's population multiplied sixfold, from approximately 12,500 to over 80,000. Along with the great torrent of immigrants came immense social changes. As immigration into the city peaked, and as Calgary society grew increasingly complex, the need for better and more numerous community services became apparent. School construction was a high priority between 1905 and 1914 due to chronic shortages in classroom space for incoming children, and to the recognized importance of a sound education system in attracting settlers to the urban frontier. Government facilities were also badly needed. Calgary's first city hall, a low, wooden frame building constructed in 1887, had long been outmoded and was hardly a fitting emblem of a proud, progressive community in a decade of unprecedented prosperity. The Land Titles Office, which was located in a humble frame structure on Eighth Avenue and Fourth Street West, and the small sandstone Court House which was erected in 1888, were likewise inadequate by 1905. The mounting pressures of urban growth thus strained the capability of existing facilities, including churches, to meet local needs. In addition, requirements for new institutions such as the public library, which was deemed essential to the development of a mature urban society, attested to the sudden change in cultural aspirations in the city.

In response to this situation, members of local school boards, officials of the municipal, provincial and federal governments, as well as zealous leaders of the community, acted to bring Calgary up to date and thus to better prepare the city for the future. The buildings which were subsequently erected met educational, administrative and community needs rather handily. Moreover, they were opulent reminders of Calgary's permanence as an established urban presence and the fact that the city shared freely in the current metropolitan culture of the Empire and North America. They also provided assurance to local residents that social, cultural and spiritual needs were being met through institutional development which continued apace with the city's material progress.

This chapter will examine institutional and public buildings erected in Calgary between 1905 and 1914. To begin with, the aggressive building campaign of the Calgary Public School board will be outlined. By far the largest and most dominant educational institution in the city, the non-sectarian public school system, played a vital role in shaping early Calgary society, in addition to overseeing the mental and moral development of children.[1] Next, the construction of new and more elaborate public buildings will be described. The government facilities, community services and churches that were erected not only accommodated the needs of local residents but also provided the community with impressive, substantial architecture that was more in keeping with Calgary's big city status.

# Public Schools[2]

During the first decade that Alberta was a province, attendance figures for Calgary's public schools paralleled the dramatic increases in the residential population of the city. In 1905 there were nearly two thousand pupils registered with the Public School Board; by 1914, close to ten thousand.

### Public School Attendance, 1906-1914

| Year | Attendance |
|------|------------|
| 1906 | 1,911 |
| 1907 | 2,527 |
| 1908 | 2,980 |
| 1909 | 3,545 |
| 1910 | 4,421 |
| 1911 | 5,800 |
| 1912 | 7,385 |
| 1913 | 8,659 |
| 1914 | 9,587 |

Source: *City of Calgary Municipal Manual*, 1915, p. 132.

To accommodate these swollen numbers, thirty-five schools were erected and numerous additions to existing structures were undertaken by the Board prior to World War I.[3] While mainly a response to actual shortages of classroom space, the ambitious building programme of the Public system was also aimed at keeping up with successive extensions of the municipal boundaries and anticipated population increases in outlying subdivisions. Explosive population growth particularly in the number of property owners in the city, had expanded the local tax base significantly, thereby allowing considerable increases in the Board's building budget. By 1914, the Public system had acquired fifty-six schools and school sites scattered across the sprawling city.[4]

The year 1905 witnessed several key developments in the Calgary Public School system. On May 24, Queen Victoria's birthday, Central School was officially opened amidst a clamour of patriotic fervour.[5] Its completion was clearly an important event, for the building represented the first fruits of an improvement policy adopted by the Board in 1903.[6] At that time, overcrowded conditions in the old Central, East Ward and South Ward schools demonstrated the inadequacy of current planning practices. It was therefore decided by the Board that elementary and high schools would henceforth be separated, that new facilities would be built, and that in the future strict attention would be paid to keeping Calgary up-to-date with educational developments.[7]

The new Central School was a credit to both the public education system and the city of Calgary. As well as relieving the attendance pressure on other schools, it was one of the most attractive sandstone buildings erected in the city up to that time in terms of its scale and design. Three storeys in height, it featured an elaborate Baroque cupola which became a noted landmark in the community. Romanesque and classical qualities were also exhibited in the bold massing of the stone, the round-arched entrance and window surround heads in the projecting frontispiece, the pedimented dormers in the roof and the heavily corbelled chimneys. When it was finished, the *Herald* confidently boasted that it was "a beautiful school, the finest west of Toronto."[9].

Central School, Calgary, c. 1900

The contract for the construction of the building was
awarded to Messieurs Addison and Davey late in 1903.[10]
On May 24, 1904, the cornerstone was laid, and work
proceeded swiftly to completion a year later.[11] Plans for the
school had originally come from Winnipeg but were
adapted to local needs by William Dodd, a Calgary
architect. However, it was decided by the Board that,
unlike the Winnipeg schools which were built of brick,
Central School would be made with local sandstone from
the McArthur quarry north of the Bow River.[12] Inside, ten
rooms, an assembly hall and a basement offered ample
space for pupils. In a word, Calgary residents were ecstatic
about their city's first large school. The *Herald* caught the
mood in a typically hyperbolic report announcing the
formal opening:

*It is doubtful if in all Canada there is a school more
complete, more up-to-date, and as handsome as the
new Calgary $75,000 school ... Every good idea, every
suggestion of experienced school men has been
carefully noted and included in this building ... [It]
stands as an ornament to the city, and justifies the
assertion that nowhere is there a prettier school than
this.*[13]

Later that same year, the School Board honoured its
commitment to the new policy of growth by announcing
plans for the construction of another large school. In mid-
December, a contract was let for the erection of a three-
storey, ten-room building on the South Ward grounds.
Haultain School, as it was known after 1910, supplemented
the original two-room stone structure following its opening
in 1907. The smaller facility was subsequently used as
office space by the newly-hired Superintendent of Schools
and his small staff.

Building operations became increasingly active after 1905,
in contrast to the almost stagnant record of previous years.
In 1906, work was started on a four-room addition to the
East Ward building. That year, the city also purchased and
offered a parcel of land—Block 18, Section 16—to the
province as the site for a teacher training school at a price
of $15,000.[14] The proposal was accepted, and plans were
soon drawn up by the Department of Public Works for the
first Normal School in Alberta.[15] Local citizens and
educators had lobbied with the territorial government for
the establishment of such an institute as early as 1902. In
November 1905, the request was acknowledged by the new
provincial government, and in January of the next year a
facility for training teachers was set up on the top floor of
Central School. There it remained until the new building
was completed. In conjunction with this venture, the
Public School Board made arrangements with provincial
administrators for the use of eight elementary school
classes in the proposed building. The agreement not only
served to lighten the burden of enrollment at other
schools, but also gave teaching students a convenient
opportunity for making classroom observations and for

practice teaching.[16]

Construction of the patiently awaited Calgary Normal School commenced in September 1906. Two years later it was ready for occupation.[17] Work was carried out slowly at first; only the concrete and sandstone masonry basement walls were in place by spring of 1907.[18] However, after the laying of the cornerstone by Premier Rutherford in June, the erection of the superstructure proceeded at a quickened pace. Legal problems with the contractor resulted in minor delays in construction, but the building was gradually brought to completion by day-labourers from the Department of Public Works.[19] In September 1908, the province's first teacher training school was formally opened.

When the magnificent Normal School was completed, the Department of Public Works declared that it was "the largest educational building finished to date in the Province, and the most pretentious one finished by the Department."[20] Built at a cost of $150,000, it was an imposing structure, three storeys high, symmetrically planned and richly detailed.[21] Above the arched entranceway was a colonnade which, together with the elegant copper cornice, flat roof line and attic storey with ornamental rondelles, gave the building a distinctive Renaissance Revival appearance. Native sandstone was used in the load-bearing walls;[22] at the basement level the stone was rusticated in contrast to the smooth-dressed upper storeys which were finely decorated with keystones, quoins, a string course and a frieze band. Inside, numerous rooms finished with plaster and oak provided ample space for instruction and practice teaching.

The building rapidly became an object of pride for Calgary residents and was frequently noted in booster literature as evidence of the city's progressive spirit. In its 1909 anniversary edition, the *Albertan* went so far as to claim that the Calgary Normal School was the "finest in the Dominion."[23] It was a monumental structure, and represented a lavish expenditure on the part of the Province. The grandeur of the building thus reflected the buoyant optimism of the government in Alberta's future growth. Furthermore, since this architectural style was currently popular in Great Britain,[24] its appearance in western Canada suggests that, among provincial administrators, Edwardian fashions were clearly favoured.[25]

Normal School, Calgary, c. 1910

With the expansion of Calgary's municipal boundaries in 1907, the Public School Board suddenly discovered that its jurisdiction had been extended in several directions. In response, a committee was struck in April to begin planning facilities for children in the new districts of Riverside, Bridgeland, Sunnyside, Hillhurst, Grand Trunk and Parkdale.[26] It was resolved, at least temporarily, that several rooms would be rented in nearby buildings until the construction of permanent facilities was approved.[27]

In addition, the year witnessed the official planning of permanent accommodation for the city's high school students. During the month of July, a contract was awarded to McDonald Roy for the erection of an eight-room sandstone school at a cost of $68,600.[28] Calgary

Collegiate Institute, as it was named, was located on Thirteenth Avenue West, close to the city's élite enclave. It represented another step in the progressive up-grading of the Public School system.

Designed by an architect who came to Calgary from Australia,[29] the building was a picturesque composition with a variety of visually interesting elements. The high-hipped roof over the central bay, pepper pots, turrets with bartizan-like mouldings, armourial shields and other medieval effects were characteristic of the Scottish Baronial style.[30] This building thus provides yet another illustration of the adoption of Anglo-Celtic architectural forms in Calgary.

Calgary Collegiate Institute, ca. 1912

No new buildings were undertaken by the Board in 1908, probably on account of the sudden worsening of the financial climate in the west.[31] But with the resurgence of the regional economy and reaffirmation of Calgary's importance as a commercial, industrial and transportation centre, construction activity accelerated. Between 1909 and 1913, the height of the building boom in Calgary, a total of 32 new schools were undertaken, including 12 sandstone, 15 two-room cottage, 2 four-room brick cottage and 3 four-room bungalow schools.[32]

In 1909, work was started on three new schools. Two of them, Langevin School located in Riverside and Mount Royal School located on Fourteenth Street and Twentieth Avenue South, were identical in plan. Both were three-storey sandstone structures with eight classrooms, and cost approximately $65,000 each to build, including land.[33] More modest in proportion was Sunnyside Cottage School, a two-storey, four-room building, the first brick school constructed by the Public School Board.[34]

The following year proved to be even more active. Connaught School, a three-storey, twelve-room building, was started after details of a contract worth $98,000 were finalized.[35] When completed, it became the largest school in Calgary. The year 1910 also witnessed the implementation of a novel policy of erecting smaller, easy-to-build cottage schools across the city. In order to keep pace with the rapidly multiplying school population, the Board resolved that numerous temporary, low-cost, wood-frame structures would be built over the course of the next few years. Most of these were two-room, two-storey buildings constructed in the bungalow style.[36] Simple, functional structures almost lacking in ornamentation, they were designed with the view that they could be converted to residential use when permanent facilities were erected[37]. Three were built that year in the districts of Hillhurst, Sunalta and East Calgary.

At the same time, however, the School Board made it clear that sandstone edifices were a definite preference. As well as giving the school system a high profile in the community, these buildings were advantageous from an economic point of view. High-quality masonry buildings were considered less of a fire hazard and had a lengthy life span of seventy-five years. This meant that sandstone schools were less risky investments for financiers. With this in mind, the Calgary Public School Board asked permission

Cottage School, Calgary, ca. 1912

from the Department of Education to extend the term of debenture bonds from thirty to forty years.[38]

In 1911, continued immigration and the further extension of the municipal boundaries underscored existing shortages of classroom space across the city. In an effort to meet immediate needs, the Building Department of the School Board began work on three sandstone and eight two-room cottage schools. Earl Grey School, located on Hillcrest Avenue and Eighth Street South, was built on the same plan as Mount Royal and Langevin schools, but at a higher cost of $97,067.[39] Two other sandstone facilities, Hillhurst and Colonel Walker in East Calgary, were similarly identical in design. Both were three-storey sandstone structures with eleven rooms, and featured a rather austere, flat roof line with a balustrade across the top, unpretentious rectangular windows and Tuscan columns in the front entrance. Somewhat plain in appearance compared to many other sandstone schools in the city, these buildings owed their design to the Connaught School, finished the year before. Meanwhile, eight cottage schools worth approximately $5,000 each were constructed in West Mount Pleasant, LaGrange, Mewata, Erlton, Grand Trunk, Sereni, North Calgary and Glengarry.[40] Although they provided much-needed space for local school children, it was still necessary for the Board to rent three church halls in Hillhurst that year, at least until the new sandstone facility was completed.[41]

In 1912, work was commenced on four additional sandstone schools. King George,[42] Ramsay and Sunalta, all duplicates in design and construction,[43] were started in June 1912, and were to be finished a year later. Each was two and a half storeys high and had fourteen classrooms which could accommodate six hundred students. A hipped roof with gable pediments located centrally in each façade, evenly spaced rectangular windows, heavy arch over the entranceway, cupola crowning the ventilation shaft, and symmetrical plan gave each school a massive and essentially classical appearance. In keeping with the requirements of the new curriculum adopted that year, each building was also fitted with manual training and domestic science facilities.[44] King Edward School, located in South Calgary, was a larger version of the same plan, with nineteen classrooms and two cupolas. It was constructed in a similar fireproof manner, with reinforced concrete, brick and sandstone.[45] These schools marked a significant change in school construction in Calgary.[46] Numerous other schools were erected in 1912. Park Hill School became the second four-room brick structure to be erected by the Board, while four two-room cottage schools were proposed and built in the growing districts of Bridgeland, Capitol Hill, Tuxedo Park and South Calgary.[47]

The school building programme was continued in 1913, despite sluggish conditions in the western Canadian economy, a general slow-down in construction work in Calgary and a rising municipal debt. In an effort to provide more space in the temporary schools, the Board halted its scheme of erecting two-room structures in favour of four-room bungalow schools. That year, three of the larger, improved design were built in the districts of Ogden, Riverside and North Mount Pleasant. In addition, the year saw the commencement of two impressive buildings in North Calgary. Bridgeland and Balmoral schools were both two-storey, fifteen-room structures designed by William A. Branton, a draftsman with the Building Department of the School Board. Bridgeland School,[48] located on Eighth Avenue and Sixth Street Northeast, was the more highly decorated of the two, indeed of all schools in the city, with its flurry of pediments, pilasters, festoons and other ostentatious classical trim.

Bridgeland School, Calgary, 1914

Although lacking the exuberant detail of Bridgeland School, Balmoral School, located on Sixteenth Avenue and First Street Northwest, was doubtless the most elegant educational facility erected by the public system during the decade. Built on a long rectangular plan, the structure was divided into five proportional bays. The central bay, which projected slightly from the rest of the building, was richly adorned with Ionic pilasters, carved lions' heads and other refined classical motifs around the entrance. Rusticated bands in the lower level gave the school a sense of strength, and contrasted with the planed stone and skillfully articulated mouldings of the upper storeys. Above the hipped and flat-topped cottage roof was a bold, black clock tower, a feature which made the school visible for miles. Balmoral School was a coherent, balanced work of remarkable craftsmanship. It was yet another example of the "stripped" or Free Classical style of architecture which was characterized by simplified but graceful form and the discreet expression of classical details.[49] This style was notably popular in Calgary prior to the war.

Balmoral School, Calgary

Plans for the Balmoral School were prepared in August 1913,[50] and within a short time construction was commenced by the contractor, J.A. McPhail.[51] Like many of the other stone schools in the city, it was considered fireproof, with reinforced concrete floors, thick sandstone and brick masonry walls[52] and a slate roof. It cost $194,545 to build, plus $37,439 for the land, and was the most expensive property investment of the Board.[53] Officially opened in September 1915, it housed both elementary and high school students from North Calgary for a time.[54] Balmoral School was the finest sandstone school erected in the city; it was also the last sandstone edifice to be completed, and hence marked the end of a fascinating era in the history of Calgary's built environment.

In summary, the decade 1905 to 1914 witnessed several important developments regarding Calgary's public schools. As a result of explosive population increases, the Public School Board was faced with an onerous task of providing proper educational facilities and quality instruction for incoming masses of school children. The challenge was met courageously. Within one short decade, the school system was transformed into a highly professional organization with its own bureaucratic administration, a staff of nearly two hundred teachers[55] and dozens of buildings and sites with an assessed value of over $4 million.[56] The sandstone schools, in particular, were the envy of many Canadian cities.[57] Most of them were built from common plans and thereby manifested the School Board's overriding concern for planning and construction efficiency, another outcome of the bureaucratic growth of the system. Generally speaking, the sandstone schools were of increasingly better design. They were successively larger, safer and better equipped with modern services deemed essential for student comfort. As well, they were progressively more expensive. Higher costs were the result of spiralling land values, increased wages for labour and the erection of more elaborate facilities. Yet while costs climbed, the incredible growth of the local population and concomitant expansion of the tax base gave the Public Board sufficient capital to construct numerous grand structures, the most noted of which were the Bridgeland and Balmoral schools.

In addition to providing much-needed accommodation for pupils, the schools played a vital role in fostering a new self-image in the city. Central, Calgary Normal, Connaught, King Edward, Calgary Collegiate, Balmoral and other sandstone schools were imposing and reserved designs. They figured prominently in the emerging skyline of the modern metropolis, and presented striking evidence to residents and visitors alike of the prosperity of the city and its rapid economic and social transformation. Moreover, these attractive and costly school buildings were an indication of the great importance assigned to education in the city. They were applauded by one English observer as well-suited to any immigrant seeking the best for his children.

> ... Happily for the generation that is knocking at the door, Calgary spares no pains and no money to perfect its education system ... Education is recognized as the great motive power of progress, and every citizen of Calgary wants his children to get the best chance ... And ... as more buildings are required they rise ...[58]

Grand Edwardian designs were particularly suited to school buildings during this period. One of the espoused aims of the public school system was to mould children, particularly non-English speaking immigrants, into patriotic subjects of the British Empire, and thereby to build the nation.[59] Teachers thus gave considerable emphasis to the inculcation of imperialist norms and moral values in academic instruction, a goal coincident with the policies and objectives of the provincial Department of Education. As Provincial School Inspector W.A. Smith once remarked to Calgary residents, "character and citizenship are the only excuses for education at public expense."[60] The erection of substantial and dignified sandstone schools appealed to the imagination of school children and thus helped to instill in their minds something of the tradition and splendour of the Empire. More important, perhaps, the schools satisfied older members of the community, notably members of the civic élite and policy makers of major institutions, that theirs was a society fundamentally British in origin and outlook, and that the destiny of western Canada lay in the continued nurturing of the imperial bond. This same spirit was manifested in many of the public buildings that were erected during the pre-war era.

# Public Buildings

Like the many schools built between 1905 and 1914, Calgary's public buildings were erected in response to the expanding needs of a rapidly mushrooming population. They exhibited many of the same trends in design and construction as the schools, and similarly, were among the most conspicuously affluent structures in the urban skyline.

Calgary's City Hall was one of the most remarkable public buildings erected in the community prior to 1914. Shrouded in controversy, the facility cost nearly $300,000, almost double the original estimate,[61] and took approximately three and a half years to bring to completion. City Hall was a constant source of embarrassment for local officials during the period of its construction, but when finished it quickly became one of the city's prized possessions. Even though it necessitated raising the mill rate fourteen and one-half mills,[62] it was applauded in the 1915 Municipal Manual as "the most modern city hall west of Toronto."[63]

Members of City Council and the architect, William Dodd, were chiefly responsible for the turmoil which developed. Early in 1907, Council authorized the expenditure of $150,000 for a municipal building and invited architects to submit proposals.[64] But when the tenders were opened, it was discovered that the lowest bid was $190,000, far above the budgeted sum.[65] Dodd, who was known for his work on Central School and the Regina City Hall, subsequently lowered his bid to $142,000 by deleting numerous items, including the furnishings and fixtures.[66] City officials agreed with his premise that, when the money had run out, a separate money by-law would be speedily passed by local ratepayers, and on that basis awarded him the contract. The Alberta Building Company was subsequently subcontracted to erect City Hall, and by August 1907 construction was under way.[67]

Work proceeded smoothly until March 1909 when the prescribed funds were exhausted. Dodd then approached the public and Council for an extra $77,000 to cover the costs of replacing the wooden floors with reinforced concrete covered with terrazzo tiles, an addition to the central tower, fixtures and furnishings.[68] Much to his surprise, he met considerable resistance. The money by-law was put to the electorate on April 20, 1909, and was soundly defeated. The situation became even more complicated when the Alberta Building Company walked off the job during the next month, charging that Dodd owed $19,502.66 for work already completed.[69] In response, Council members threatened to get rid of the construction company for failing to prosecute the work responsibly and diligently, as specified in the contract.[70]

As a means of resolving the embroglio, an investigation was begun by Council to review the whole affair. The General Appraisal Company, an independent firm from Seattle, was subsequently hired to submit an evaluation of the disputed construction work. Interestingly, the company reported that Dodd had actually overpaid the contractor.[71] As a result, Dodd was lampooned by the local press and was further ridiculed when he tried to defend himself.[72] Members of City Council found themselves in an appalling tangle with a half-finished building, an irresponsible builder, an architect believed to be incompetent and an irate citizenry. Probably more as a convenient way out of a sticky situation than a strict judgement of professional credibility, the special committee on City Hall recommended to Council that William Dodd be fired as supervising architect of the project on December 18, 1909.[73]

Work on the structure could not resume, however, until the required money was obtained in another plebiscite. This time, though, the Calgary *Herald* carefully urged the ratepayers to support the money by-law.[74] On May 25, 1910, the by-law was passed and the building was pressed onward to completion. Within almost a year, it was ready to be used; covered with a host of banners, it was officially opened on June 26, 1911, by Robert L. Borden, leader of the federal Opposition.

City Hall was an impressive addition to the growing list of magnificent sandstone buildings in Calgary. It was a robust, three-storey structure with a projecting central clock tower nearly seventy feet in height. The bold texture and heavy massing of the stone gave it a powerful sense of gravity, a highly appropriate quality for a municipal government facility where the interests of citizens were scrupulously pondered by local policy makers. The external style of the building was Romanesque Revival, characterized by an overall ruggedness, rounded-arched windows and entrance, a heavily dentilled cornice and a general avoidance of light ornamentation. Gable dormers crowned with raised lanterns on the corners, and a steeply pitched roof gave it the appearance of a medieval

City Hall, Calgary, ca. 1911

fortification, a character which was further reinforced by the placement of cannons around the entrance shortly after it was opened. In many respects, the style of City Hall was similar to that of numerous sandstone buildings erected on Eighth Avenue during the late 1880s and 1890s. It also resembled an earlier work of Dodd's, Central School, which was completed in 1905. City Hall may thus be viewed as a conservative or retardataire design, unlike some of the progressive, rationalized structures built at the same time. It was, however, comparable in construction to many of the city's finest schools with its reinforced concrete floors, internal steel beams and thick sandstone walls backed with brick masonry.[76]

Land Titles building, Calgary, ca. 1930

The Land Titles Building, started during the same year, provided a distinct contrast in design and finish to City Hall. It was refined, almost chaste in appearance: the smooth-faced sandstone in the main storeys blended well with the rubble stone in the basement walls, giving the structure a quiet, formal character.[77] The highlight of the building was the front façade. Twenty-three granite steps led up to the square doorway, which was set in a semicircular arch. Above that was a pediment which bore the provincial seal moulded in high relief, and which was supported by two Ionic columns and projecting pilasters. These and other decorative elements revealed that the building was designed in a rationalized, Free Classical style[78].

Located on Seventh Avenue between Fourth and Fifth Streets West, the Land Titles Building was the first major public edifice undertaken by the provincial government in Calgary. Construction commenced in 1907, following the completion of the drawings by the Department of Public Works.[79] Unlike Calgary's City Hall, though, the building was virtually ready for occupation by the end of 1908, as scheduled,[80] and at a more reasonable cost of $80,000.[81] Strict attention was paid throughout to make this one of the most fireproof buildings in Alberta. The exterior walls were made of Calgary sandstone backed with brick and concrete, while steel beams and reinforced concrete provided the principal internal support for the floors, posts and roof.[82] Hollow terra cotta furring blocks were used to line the inside of the masonry walls as protection against moisture and possible fire. Various storerooms, a large public area and offices for the Registrar, Deputy Registrar and clerical assistants were located inside, as well as numerous large vaults where precious legal records and documents were stored. The rooms and corridors were carefully finished with non-flammable materials such as plaster, wrought iron, terra cotta, marble and rubberized tile. The only wood to be found in the entire structure was in the exterior windows and doors. Even the heating system was designed to minimize the chances of accidental fire: steam was brought into the building through pipes from an outside generating station.[83] Such precautions in construction were viewed as absolutely necessary for the safe-keeping of an expanding mass of vital land transfer records in this, the most frenetic period of development in Calgary's history.

Within a few years, a second building was erected by the Department of Public Works alongside the Land Titles Building. Calgarians knew of the proposed Court House as early as May 1909.[84] However, because of apparent cutbacks in the Department's budget, plans for the edifice were not finished until 1912.[85] Construction was started shortly thereafter, and by the end of the year all the steel work was erected and all of the stone work, with the exception of the front entrance, was completed.[86] In 1913, the plumbing and steam heating systems were installed and the marble and tile work was finished, but it was not until the following year that the building was ready for use.

Court House, Calgary, ca. 1930

The new Court House was similar in appearance to the Land Titles Building. It was the same height and was also built of Calgary stone, which was smooth-dressed in the upper storeys and rock-faced at the basement level.[87] Like the Land Titles Building, it was also fashioned in the Free Classical style. But unlike the adjacent structure, the Court House was constructed on a long, rectangular plan. It was an austere building with a minimum of decorative detail. The most interesting aspect of the main façade was the central bay in which the arched entranceway was contained, and above which was a colonnade-like arrangement of Tuscan columns. It was, however, an essentially well-proportioned and pleasing design. Evenly

108

spaced rectangular windows and a heavy parapet gave it a strong sense of unity, while the double string course between the first and second storeys mollified the building's apparent severity. The structure was unassuming and serious in character, and thus suitably designed for use as a Court House. Variously estimated at between $185,000 and $300.000,[88] it offered members of the judiciary, administrators and clerical staff the expanded and fully modern services that were needed to handle the multiplying number of court cases that were heard in Calgary.

Besides the government buildings, numerous community services were constructed in the city to keep pace with the growing needs of local residents. Among these were the new General Hospital[89] and the Salvation Army Building, finished in 1909, the Young Men's Christian Association Building , which cost $95,000 and was opened the same year, the Young Women's Christian Association Building started in 1910,[90] a new and massive police headquarters, and numerous firehalls spread across the city.

Fire Hall Number One became the new headquarters for the Fire Department upon its completion in 1911. Designed by local architects Lang and Major,[91] it was a striking yet functional building. Five large bays at ground level allowed easy movement of the modern motorized fleet of fire engines,[92] while the angular placement of the structure on its site permitted rapid access to either street or avenue in the event of a fire. The visibility of Fire Hall Number One was further enhanced by its conspicuously Renaissance Revival styling, and the use of sandstone trim around the windows and arched bays as a material and chromatic contrast.

Of the new community services erected in the city, the most outstanding architectural work was the monumental Public Library. Funded almost entirely by Andrew Carnegie, the benevolent Pittsburgh steel magnate, it was the first library in Calgary, indeed in Alberta. Carnegie pledged his financial support for the project on March 21, 1908, in response to a plea sent by Mr. E.L. Hill, Alderman A.J. Samis and a local women's group.[93] Following that, the first library board, which included such notable citizens as R.B. Bennett, Alderman Samis, Reverend J.A. Clark and Mr. Hill, was appointed to oversee the establishment of the institution. The City of Calgary subsequently agreed to donate land for the building worth $20,000, and on August 12, 1908, a site was chosen in Central Park by the citizens in a plebiscite.[94]

Main Fire Hall, Calgary, ca. 1912

Early in September 1909, a contract worth $67,650 was awarded to R.A. Brocklebank for the construction of the edifice.[95] Brocklebank, who had been active in municipal politics as an alderman, resigned from his post to take full charge of the project which was to be completed by Thanksgiving Day, 1910.[96] In October, the excavation was done and construction work commenced. However, due to minor complications, the building was not ready for more than a year after the deadline. On January 2, 1912, the library was opened to the public, and ten days later, the first books were loaned out.[97] Following the inaugural ceremony on April 26, 1912, it instantly became one of the most celebrated cultural centres in the city.

Public Library, Calgary, ca. 1915

Calgary's Public Library was a masterpiece in both design and craftsmanship. It was a compact, two-storey structure, built with load-bearing sandstone walls backed with brick.[98]. Smoothly finished stone, decorated window surround heads, balconies off the largest rectangular windows in the first storey, latticing in the smaller second storey windows and other ornamental details which crowned the low-hipped roof gave it a stately yet festive air. The classically inspired portico was the central feature of the main facade. Set on top of a series of granite steps, the temple-like arrangement of Ionic columns and skillfully carved pediment drew attention to the building and acted as an effective preparation for entry into the dignified atmosphere of the library. Inside, the ornate

**111**

embellishment was repeated in the moulded ceiling, plaster columns and birch trim. Calgary's Carnegie Library was designed in the Free Classical style by McLean and Wright, architects from Boston, Massachusetts. It showed strong influence of the Beaux-Arts tradition, a French school of architecture which had an enormous impact on public building design in both the United States and Great Britain, and which was characterized by disciplined and beautiful forms, elegant ornamentation and scenically planned grounds.[99]

The Public Library was one of the most lavish structures in the city. It was only the second library between Winnipeg and the Rocky Mountains,[100] and thus must have given local residents a great sense of prestige for having warranted the blessing of Mr. Andrew Carnegie. Altogether, the building and equipment cost $100,000: of this sum, $80,000 had come from the Pittsburgh millionaire and $20,000 was donated by the City of Calgary.[101] Close to five thousand volumes had been amassed by the librarian, Alexander Calhoun, when the facility first opened; by the end of 1913, nearly twenty thousand were available for Calgary's readers. They suddenly found themselves inundated with good literature which was, in the words of one booster, "a sure sign of permanent progress"[102] in the city.

Yet the library was more than a mere shelter for books. It was, perhaps more important, a vital educational and cultural centre where local groups such as the Calgary Natural History Society and the Calgary Arts Association met regularly,[103] and where the first classes of the infant University of Calgary were held. It was also a place where school children and adults alike ventured to obtain reading material, where art collections, historical artifacts and Indian curios were displayed, and where special lectures were often heard. Although the sort of culture that was nurtured there may have appealed more to residents of the exclusive district surrounding Central Park, the Calgary Public Library proved itself a welcome addition to the city, and became a symbol of an increasingly sophisticated and cosmopolitan life style of Calgary residents in this decade of unparalleled growth.

Churches, too, proliferated in the boom years. In 1906, the *Herald* noted that there were eleven churches in the city;[104] by 1914, over seventy were counted.[105] Most were designed in the Gothic Revival style, an architectural form that was unquestionably identified with Christian institutions in the Anglo-Celtic tradition, especially during the Victorian era when the aesthetic ideals of A.W.N. Pugin and John Ruskin held enormous sway. Since a large proportion of Calgary residents were of British extraction, and since many of the major Protestant denominations retained ties with the old country, the appearance of traditional Gothic churches in the city was almost to be expected. Among the most noted of these structures were: the Anglican Church of the Redeemer, a massive, low-lying structure which became the temporary cathedral in 1905;[106] Central Methodist Church, another bulky sandstone edifice completed the same year; St. Barnabas Presbyterian Church, designed by Leo Dowler and constructed on a site in Hillhurst donated by E.H. Riley;[107] Hillhurst Presbyterian Church, an interesting design which combined a Gothic plan with half-timbering;[108] Christchurch, another Anglican facility designed by Lang and Major, and constructed in 1913 on a site given by another famous landowner, Fred Lowes;[109] Grace Presbyterian Church, designed in 1913 by Smith and Gemmel, noted church architects from Toronto;[110] First Baptist Church, renowned for its prominent spire; and Knox Presbyterian Church, perhaps the most magnificent church of the decade.

First Baptist Church was one of the first congregations in Calgary. Organized in 1888, it grew from a mere handful of members to one of the city's largest religious communities. By 1906, five new congregations had been formed from the membership of First Baptist, including the Westbourne, Heath, Olivet, Hillhurst and Crescent Heights Baptist churches.[111] Numerous facilities were erected for the swelling number of people who attended services at First Baptist Church. The first building, erected in 1890, seated 125 people; the last one, formally dedicated on May 12, 1912, had a seating capacity of 1,360.[112] When completed, the *Herald* described it as "one of the finest churches in western Canada."[113]

The new First Baptist Church, located on Thirteenth
Avenue and Fourth Street West, was an immense structure
compared to its predecessors. Designed by D.S. McIlroy, it
was built of red brick with sandstone trim by the Richards
Brothers Company.[114] The total cost of the church and
manse was $157,000.[115] Large stained-glass windows
which illustrated Biblical truths, steeply pitched gables,
a saddleback roof and an octagonal spire 125 feet
high covered with copper shingles gave it a traditional
appearance with a considerable vertical emphasis. The
interior was, by contrast, fully adopted to modern
purposes. It included a large sanctuary finished with oak
and brass fixtures, a baptistry lined with white marble, a
spacious Sunday School hall with thirteen classes, a dining
hall which could seat five hundred people, a kitchen and a
storeroom. Attention was paid to the ventilation, cleaning,
heating and plumbing systems to make the building as
comfortable as possible for visitors.[116] First Baptist Church
was thus a combination of a traditional form with the
latest in building services, a composition of architectural
beauty and modern utility.

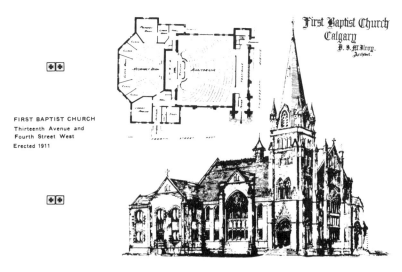

FIRST BAPTIST CHURCH
Thirteenth Avenue and
Fourth Street West
Erected 1911

Architectural drawing and plan of First Baptist Church, Calgary, 1911

114

Knox Presbyterian Church, Calgary

Another of the many handsome ecclesiastical structures built during the city's boom years was Knox Presbyterian Church. As in the case of First Baptist Church, four facilities had to be erected for the Knox congregation because of the constant growth in attendance since it was started in 1883.[115] The last and largest of these was constructed between 1911 and 1913 on the corner of Sixth Avenue and Fourth Street West at a cost of $205,000.[118] According to Reverend J.A. Clark, the move from Seventh Avenue and Center Street was necessary because most of the congregation lived in the western sector of the city, because of the rapid encroachment of the business district and, finally, because east Calgary was filling up with foreigners.[119] Plans for the new church were initially drawn up by an architectural firm from Boston, Massachusetts.[120] They were, however, rejected by members in April 1911, and the building committee was then instructed to find a local architect for the job. In May, the design submitted by Frank J. Lawson, a Scottish-trained architect,[121] was accepted, and by the end of the year work was well under way. On September 21, 1912, the cornerstone was laid, and almost a year later the church was dedicated.[122]

Knox Presbyterian Church was a skillfully executed work. Sandstone from the Bone and LeBlanc quarry in Shaganappi was cut into polygonal blocks of various sizes and smooth-dressed before it was set into the walls of the building.[123] Also of note were the elaborate perpendicular tracery, the tall and massive square tower with crenelated parapet, and the system of buttresses.[124] The Gothic motif was continued inside in the long nave and spacious choir, where a total of twelve hundred people could be seated.[125] Knox Presbyterian Church was an austere yet refined edifice. In spite of grave problems experienced in financing the building, the church gained a reputation as one of the finest places of worship in western Canada.

\*     \*     \*

The numerous public schools, government facilities, community services and churches built between 1905 and 1914 were highly important in obliterating the last vestiges of Calgary's humble origins and in creating a new, cosmopolitan self-image for the city. These buildings not only provided more and better services to the growing population, but also added a sense of richness and prestige to the urban environment. Baroque, Romanesque, Classical and Renaissance Revival, Free Classical and other architectural forms presented a visually eclectic landscape that was characteristic of much older centres in North America and the United Kingdom. Calgary society had changed a great deal since 1875, or even 1895; the buildings reflected this change in their increased size and grandeur. By 1914, Calgary had become one of the most fiercely competitive and prosperous, as well as one of the most educationally and culturally accomplished cities in western Canada. Local boosters and reporters may well have tended to be uncritical in their descriptions of Calgary's new buildings, but the fact remained that nowhere on the Canadian plains was there a city that was rising to prominence as energetically as Calgary.

The many schools and public buildings that were erected during this decade of affluence also revealed the persistence of certain cultural ties. Although extensive immigration altered the city's population structure after

1905, Calgary society remained predominantly British in orientation. Class distinctions and ethnic diversity became more noticeable with the influx of vast numbers of Americans and Europeans. Nevertheless, the essential focus of Calgary, indeed western Canadian society, continued to be British,[124] a trend which was underscored by the social, cultural and political affiliations of the community's principal leaders and administrators. Loyalty to things British not only meant a devotion to a way of life that was aimed at preserving a civilized and peaceful social order.It was also manifested in the adoption of architectural fashions that were current in Great Britain, namely Gothic motifs for church buildings and Edwardian Free Classical forms for government and educational facilities. This aesthetic inclination is not surprising, however, since a large percentage of recent immigrants including architects and craftsmen, were of British extraction. The choice of formal designs for Calgary's institutional buildings by local and provincial government architects was furthermore appropriate, as they helped reinforce public attitudes of respect and order—attitudes that were fundamental to Canadian and British society in the period before World War I.

# Notes

[1]See Raymond Huel, "The Public School as Guardian of Anglo-Saxon Traditions: The Saskatchewan Experience, 1913-1918," in *Ethnic Canadians—Culture and Education,* ed. Martin L. Kovacs (Regina: Canadian Plains Research Center, 1978), pp. 295-302. See also David Bourdon. "The Empire and the Alberta School System, 1905-1914" (Unpublished seminar paper, University of Calgary, Department of History, April 1980). Also see Neil G. McDonald, "The School as an Agent of Nationalism in the North-West Territories, 1884-1905" (Unpublished M.Ed. thesis, University of Alberta, 1971); and *ibid.,* "Canadian Nationalism and North-West Schools, 1884-1905," in *Canadian Schools and Canadian Identity,* ed. A. Chaiton and

N. McDonald (Toronto: Gage Educational Publishing, Ltd., 1977), pp. 59-87.

[2] *Mea culpa.* The exclusion of the Separate School Board in this discussion is not meant to suggest that it was unimportant in Calgary's early educational development. The fact remains, however, that only three separate schools were erected in this decade, while thirty-five were built by the Public system. The student population of the Separate Board increased from 140 in 1906 to 843 in 1914, but this achievement was less than one-tenth of the population of the Public Schools. (See *Municipal Manual,* 1915, p. 132). The Separate Board furthermore obtained its first school property in September 1906, but it was not until April 1, 1909, that a contract was let for construction of the Board's first building, St. Mary's Girls' School. Only two other contracts for schools were let by the Board before the war: one for St. Anne's School in East Calgary, and the other for Sacred Heart School in Bankview. Both schools were four-room, brick structures and both were opened in January 1912. Despite the fact that classroom space was still a problem, it was not until September 1915 that the Board had sufficient financing to continue its building programme. See W.W. Barry, *An Anecdotal History of the Calgary Separate School Board* (Calgary: Calgary Separate Board, 1967), and J.W. Van Tighem, *A History of the Calgary School Board Researched From Old Records,* n.p., n.d. for more specific information.

[3] Leroi A. Daniels, "The History of Education in Calgary" (Unpublished M.Ed. thesis, University of Washington, 1954), pp. 46-62. Also Calgary Public School Board Records (hereafter cited as CPSB), "Report on Older Schools," 1951, pp. 30-38.

[4] *Municipal Manual,* 1914, p. 132

[5] *Herald,* May 23, 1905. See Robert M. Stamp, "Empire Days in the Schools of Ontario: The Training of Young Imperialists," in *Canadian Schools,* ed. Chaiton and McDonald, pp. 100-115, for a study of Empire Day patriotism and imperialist values in public education in a region from which many Calgary residents had emigrated.

[6]See Robert M. Stamp, "The Response of Urban Growth: The Bureaucratization of Public Education in Calgary, 1884-1914," in *Frontier Calgary*, ed. Rasporich and Klassen, pp. 161-164.

[7]*Ibid.*

[8]See *Herald*, May 25, 1904.

[9]*Herald*, May 23, 1905.

[10]Phyllis E. Weston, "The History of Education in Calgary" (Unpublished Master's thesis, University of Alberta, 1951), p. 22; quoted from Calgary School Board documents, December 1903.

[11]*Herald*, May 25, 1904.

[12]*Herald*, May 23, 1905. Also Weston, "History of Education in Calgary," p. 22.

[13]*Ibid.* According to CPSB, "Upgrading Report," March 1960, the actual cost of the land was $8,400.

[14]Daniels, "Education in Calgary," p. 49. Also CPSB, "Letter from G.G. White, Information Officer," May 4, 1967.

[15]The designer of the building is not known, although A.M. Jeffers, the Provincial Architect from 1908 to 1912, made reference to this person as his "predecessor in office." *Annual Report of the Provincial Department of Public Works of the Province of Alberta*, 1908 (Edmonton: Government Printer, 1909), p. 60 (hereafter cited as *DPW Report*).

[16]Weston, "History of Education in Calgary," p. 24. Also *Thompson-Tregillus Directory*, 1913, p. 144.

[17]*DPW Report*, 1908, pp. 60-62.

[18]*Ibid.*

[19]*Ibid.*

[20]*Ibid.*

[21]*Albertan*, March 1, 1909, Anniversary Edition.

[22]According to the City of Calgary, PHSE, vol. 4, category 19, file 182, the sandstone walls are four feet thick.

[23]*Albertan*, March 1, 1909, Anniversary Edition.

[24]See Alastair Service, *Edwardian Architecture*, pp. 140-169, for a discussion of Classical styles in Great Britain during the Edwardian period.

[25]As an indication of the importance of educational matters to the newly established provincial government, Premier A.C. Rutherford assumed the portfolio of education in addition to his other duties. See MacRae, *History of the Province of Alberta*, vol. 1, p. 457.

[26]Daniels, "Education in Calgary," p. 50.

[27]*Ibid.*
[28]Weston, "History of Education in Calgary," p. 24.

[29]GAI, Charles Ursenbach, "Interview with William A. Branton," February 12, and March 4, 1974, p. 4. It is possible this man was R.G. Gordon, who worked as an architect in Melbourne, Australia, before coming to Calgary. See *Henderson's Directory*, 1906, advertisements. However, according to a photograph in the December 1909 edition of *Construction*, the architect of the Calgary High School was D.S. McIlroy. Another possible architect of the high school was G.M. Lang. He is given credit for the structure in MacRae, *History of the Province of Alberta*, vol. 2, pp. 1021-1022.

[30]This style was popularized across Canada by the Canadian Pacific Railway, and later by the Canadian National Railway and the federal government. See Harold Kalman, *The Railway Hotels and the Development of the Chateau Style in Canada* (Victoria: University of Victoria and the Maltwood Museum, 1968).

[31]Back in 1906, the School Board issued debenture bonds worth $90,000 for a term of thirty years at 4.5 percent interest per annum. In 1908, they were offered at a more attractive rate of 6 percent and over a less risky period of ten years. See CPSB, "Debenture Issues of the Board, 1887 to 1924," May 18, 1925. The fact that only $9,000 worth of bonds were issued, even at a more lucrative rate, suggests that there was an uneasiness in the investment market and perhaps a lack of capital in the city in 1908.

120

[32]See Daniels, "Education in Calgary," pp. 52-60. In addition to these projects, substantial additions were built onto Central Collegiate and Victoria School. See pp. 56-57.

[33]CPSB, "Upgrading Report," March 1960.

[34]CPSB, "Report on Older Schools," 1951.

[35]See Daniels, "Education in Calgary." See also CPSB, "Report on Older Schools," 1951.

[36]See Chapter 2, section on working-class dwellings.

[37]CPSB, "Report on Older Schools," 1951.

[38]CPSB, School Board *Minutes*, March 10, 1910.

[39]CPSB, "Upgrading Report," March 1960.

[40]*Ibid.* Also Daniels, "Education in Calgary," p. 56.

[41]*Ibid.*

[42]According to W.A. Branton, stone for King George School came from a quarry near Lethbridge, while stone for most of the other schools from this period was taken from the Oliver quarry, on Seventeenth Avenue and Summit Street West. See GAI, Ursenbach, "Interview with William A. Branton," p. 5.

[43]*News Telegram*, February 22, 1913.

[44]*Ibid.* See Daniels, "Education in Calgary," pp. 133-138, for details about the new curriculum.

[45]*Ibid.*

[46]See GAI, Ursenbach, "Interview with William A. Branton," pp. 5-6.

[47]Daniels, "Education in Calgary," p. 57.

[48]It was renamed Stanley Jones School after World War I, in memory of a Calgary army officer killed in combat in France. See GAI, Ursenbach, "Interview with William A. Branton," p. 4.

[49]Service, *Edwardian Architecture*, pp. 140, 186, 187.

[50]CPSB, Architectural Services.

[51]GAI, Photo Archives.

[52]CPSB, Architectural Services, Mr. George Reddekopp and Mr. Dick Gauer.

[53]CPSB, "Upgrading Report," March 1960.

[54]Daniels, "Education in Calgary," p. 62.

[55]See Robert M. Stamp, "The Response to Urban Growth," in *Frontier Calgary*, ed. Rasporich and Klassen, p. 167.

[56]CPSB. "List of Properties," December 31, 1913.

[57]See *News Telegram*, January 19, 1909; also *Albertan*, January 2, 1911.

[58]S.L. Bensusan, ed., *Calgary* (London: Hodder and Stoughton, 1912), pp. 26, 28, 29.

[59]See Bensusan, *Calgary*, p. 26; also see *Herald*, December 26, 1906.

[60]*Herald*, January 5, 1912.

[61]*Albertan*, April 13, 1911.

[62]*Ibid.*

[63]*Municipal Manual*, 1915, p. 13.

[64]*Herald*, April 16, 1909.

[65]*Albertan*, April 19, 1909.

[66]*Ibid.*

[67]See *Albertan*, May 20, 1909, for the comments of Mr. Davey.

[68]See *Albertan*, March 24 and April 19, 1909.

[69]*Herald*, May 18, 1909.

[70]*Herald*, May 20 and 27, 1909.

[71]*Herald*, November 1, 1909.

[72]Dodd was first attacked by the *Albertan* on June 16, 1909, following an incident with a reporter. After it was discovered that he had not acted competently in paying the contractors, he was taken to task by other members of the press who generally opposed exorbitant spending. See *Herald*, November 2 and December 13, 1909, for details.

[73] *Herald*, December 18, 1909.

[74] *Herald*, May 23, 1910.

[75] *Albertan*, June 27, 1911.

[76] GAI, Original Plans of City Hall; also *Herald*, December 18, 1909. Dodd also designed the Regina City Hall, which bore a remarkable resemblance to the Calgary facility, except for the use of brick. See *Construction* 8, no. 1 (November 1915), photographs. It was completed in 1907 according to E.J. Gilbert, *Up the Years with the Saskatchewan Association of Architects* (n.p.: The Saskatchewan Association of Architects, 1970), pp. 8, 9.

[77] *DPW Report*, 1908, pp. 62-65.

[78] *Ibid.*

[79] The architect of the Land Titles Building was probably A.M. Jeffers, Provincial Architect at the time. *DPW Reports*, 1908-1912, *passim.*

[80] *DPW Report*, 1908, pp. 72-73.

[81] *Albertan*, February 28, 1910.

[82] *DPW Report*, 1908, pp. 62-65.

[83] *Ibid.*

[84] *Herald*, May 12, 1909.

[85] *DPW Report*, 1911, p. 36. According to Edward Mills, *Court Houses of Alberta*, pp. 17-19, disclosures in 1911 of serious over-subscription in railway and irrigation company securities by the Provincial government resulted in a more scrupulous approach to public expenditures during the following years. R.P. Blakey, who took over as Provincial Architect in 1912, modified Calgary's Court House plans in an effort to reduce building costs; hence the delay in its construction.

[86] *DPW Reports*, 1912, p. 39.

[87] GAI, Photo Archives.

[88] In *Calgary in Sandstone*, p. 24, Richard Cunniffe reports that the new court house was to have cost $185,000. On

May 12, 1909, the *Herald* stated that the new structure was estimated to be worth between $250,000 and $300,000. The actual cost of the structure was tabulated in 1914 by the Department of Public Works at $280,830.15. See Edward Mills, *Court Houses of Alberta*, p. 54. Quoted from the Department of Public Works Public Accounts Records, Provincial Archives of Alberta, #70.414, box 5.

[89] *Herald*, August 21, 1909.

[90] *Albertan*, March 1, 1909.

[91] Other stations located in Victoria Park and East Calgary were designed by Lang and Major. See *Herald*, April 27, 1912.

[92] GAI, Fire Department Papers, File 10.

[93] *Herald*, April 27, 1912.

[94] *Ibid.*

[95] *Herald*, September 3, 1909.

[96] *Ibid.*

[97] *Herald*, April 27, 1912

[98] GAI, Photo Archives.

[99] See John Burchard and Albert Bush-Brown, *The Architecture of America: A Social and Cultural History* (Boston: Little, Brown, and Company, 1961), pp. 246-250, for a discussion of Beaux-Arts ideas in American architecture. The influence of the Ecole des Beaux-Arts ideas was felt for at least two decades before the turn of the century in the United States. Architects who were trained in Paris returned to the United States with a strong sense of disciplined composition. In Great Britain, the acceptance of French aesthetic notions was slower, owing to the revival of Baroque fashions. By 1906, however, there was a general move towards refinement in British Classical architecture, partly in reaction against the flamboyance of earlier years. As a result, Beaux-Arts ideas, with their emphasis on simplified, symmetrical form and elegant, almost chaste use of classical decoration, became the vogue in Edwardian Britain. See Alastair Service, *Edwardian*

*Architecture*, pp. 140, 158-169.

[100]*Henderson's Directory*, 1913, p. 134.

[101]*Ibid.*

[102]Bensusan. *Calgary*, p. 71.

[103]*Herald*, April 27, 1912.

[104]*Herald*, April 11, 1906.

[105]*Municipal Manual*, 1915 p. 170. *Mea Culpa*. Except for brief, episodic mention of several structures in the local newspapers, little historical information is apparently available on many of Calgary's smaller churches. Hence, for this study, the sample of buildings examined has been restricted to the city's most substantial ecclesiastical edifices.

[106]See David Carter, *Calgary's Anglican Cathedral* (Calgary: The Cathedral Church of the Redeemer, 1973), pp. 15-21.

[107]*Herald*, April 25, 1912.

[108]*Herald*, January 18, 1913.

[109]*Herald*, January 3, 1913.

[110]See Eric Arthur, *Toronto: No Mean City* (Toronto: University of Toronto Press, 1964), Appendix, for a list of works done by Smith and Gemmel.

[111]*Herald*, May 11, 1912.

[112]*Ibid.*

[113]*Ibid.*

[114]*Facts of Interest: Past and Present, First Baptist Church, Calgary, Alberta* (Calgary: n.pub., 1911).

[115]*Herald*, May 11, 1912

[116]*Ibid.*

[117]*A Souvenir of the Seventieth Anniversary of Knox United Church*, (Calgary: n.pub., 1953).

[118]*Herald*, September 13, 1913.

[119]*Albertan*, January 19, 1911.

[120]*Albertan*, April 25, 1911.

[121]Lawson was trained by Alex Ross of Inverness, Scotland before he came to Canada. See A.O. MacRae, *History of Alberta*, vol. 2, pp. 1015-16. Ross apparently had a considerable reputation in northern Scotland. In *Old Inverness in Pictures* (Edinburgh: Inverness Field Club and Paul Harris Publishing, 1978), photograph number 171, he is mentioned as "The Sir Christopher Wren of the North."

[122]*Herald*, September 13, 1913.

[123]Alberta Culture Historic Sites Service, file R76S.

[124]Gregory Utas, "Calgary Architect," p. 69

[125]*Herald*, September 13, 1913.

[126]Lewis G. Thomas, "Alberta Perspectives, 1905," *Alberta History* 28 (Winter 1980): 1-5.

# 4.

# Commercial Buildings

Between 1905 and 1914, Calgary took shape as a prominent commercial metropolis primarily through the growth of wheat farming in outlying areas, the convergence of numerous railways in the district, and the subsequent establishment of wholesale and retail facilities and industrial complexes. Generally and increasingly, the community developed into a major service depot and transportation hub, which acted as a processing, marketing and financial centre for the swelling number of settlers in both the agricultural hinterland and within the city. Immigration reached a high point and business activity flourished in Calgary, particularly during the boom years when grain markets continued to expand and capital investment from British, Canadian and American sources intensified.

Rapid growth in the local economy brought unforeseen changes to the urban environment. Calgary was, by 1914, a sprawling metropolis, bustling with energy and totally caught up in the excitement of its own commercial development and real estate speculation. The acceleration of business growth created problems, however, as existing facilities were either occupied or too inadequate to be used by incoming establishments. There was an especially dire shortage of prime office space to accommodate the vast number of investment brokerages, insurance agencies, real estate companies, management firms, consultants and professional corporations which were being located in Calgary. As land values skyrocketed in the central business district, and the prospect of lucrative profits from the leasing of commercial property loomed large, local entrepreneurs and eastern-based corporations alike commissioned the erection of commodious business buildings in the modern styles recently pioneered in the United States. It was thus not long before Calgary's skyline was darkened by structures six to ten storeys in height.

Outside the downtown core, commercial activity was increasingly noticeable after 1909. Small businesses began to spring up across the city, providing goods and services to residents in well-populated suburbs. As well, municipally sponsored inducements for industrial development in the southeast sector proved quite successful in attracting investors to Calgary.

This chapter will examine some of the most important developments in Calgary's commercial architecture from the period 1905 to 1914. First, the construction of large and impressive business buildings in the downtown area will be described. These new structures were vital in facilitating commercial expansion in the city. Yet even more significant, they became symbols of a progressing and prosperous era which heralded Calgary's emergence into the modern world of trade and commerce. Second, smaller commercial structures and industrial buildings in outlying districts will be discussed. Calgary's phenomenal growth in population not only gave rise to the establishment of small businesses in the suburbs, but also made the city an attractive location for industrial development. This in turn added thousands to the local residential population, which subsequently led to the construction of other manufacturing plants and business facilities. As in preceding chapters, selected buildings will be studied.

# Major Business Buildings

Calgary entered into the most dynamic period of economic expansion in its short history at the same time that large-scale settlement of surrounding rural lands was taking place. Intensive agricultural development created a demand for skills, supplies and services that could be filled only by a thriving metropolis. Calgary's early origin as the centre of ranching in the west thus virtually assured it a vital role once farming became a dominant activity. With the establishment of a large number of wholesale and retail outlets for farm implements, hardware, building materials, and other goods, Calgary subsequently emerged as the most important distributing centre west of Winnipeg. Agricultural development furthermore entailed the investment of enormous sums of capital to finance the construction of new railway lines, irrigation works, grain handling and marketing facilities, food processing plants and other industries associated with cereal or mixed farming in the hinterland. Calgary thus became a financial hub as well, as banks, mortgage companies, insurance agencies, land companies, investment brokerages and other institutions streamed into the city to oversee and coordinate this development. Once started, commercial activity began to snowball, as both industries and service-oriented businesses connected with urban growth were set up to look after the needs of the burgeoning community. With the sudden increase in the local population and the continuation of buoyant economic conditions, business activity flourished, thereby bringing the city into an intense period of building construction and real estate speculation. As a result, Calgary was rapidly transformed into a modern metropolis, similar in appearance and character to the dominant urban centres to the east.

Evidence of Calgary's commercial diversification could certainly be seen in the central business district during the years when the boom was in full swing. Early in 1909, both International Harvester and Tees and Persse announced plans to build four-storey, solid brick warehouses.[1] By June, work was started on the Ashdown Hardware Company's four-storey warehouse on Eleventh Avenue West, and on Dr. T.H. Blow's three-storey warehouse on Eighth Avenue West, which was later occupied by O.S. Chapin and Company.[2] Numerous structures were built for apparently speculative purposes that year, including the Bailey Brothers Building and the Samis Block on Eighth Avenue East, while the Grain Exchange Building on Ninth Avenue West was erected to house the newly established grain-marketing industry in the city.[3]

Calgary's commercial development accelerated in response to the city's gigantic growth and the successive unfolding of western Canada's economic fortunes. In 1910, a total of 16 warehouses worth $362,520, 14 business blocks worth $421,200 and a department store worth $60,000 were erected,[4] including the Leeson and Lineham Block, the Nielson Block and the Lineham Building. The following year, 82 buildings worth between $10,000 and $100,000, 14 buildings worth between $100,000 and $1 million, and 2 buildings worth over $1 million were started. Among these were the Bruner Block, the Maclean Block, the Lougheed

Building, the Beveridge Block, the Burns Building, and Alexandra Hotel, the King George Hotel, the Palliser Hotel, the Pryce-Jones department store and the Hudson's Bay Company store.[5] In 1912, commercial development reached a peak: that year, 109 business buildings worth $4,402,920 and 52 warehouses and factories valued at $2,271,200 were commenced.[6] Included in this total were the Molsons' Bank, the Travellers Building, the Mackie Building, the McDougall and Forster warehouse, the Canada Life Assurance Building and the Herald Building. The year 1913 was anticlimactic by comparison, as few commercial buildings of note were constructed owing to a general slow down in the regional economy. Perhaps the biggest accomplishment was the completion of most of the substantial edifices started in 1911 and 1912. But despite depressed economic conditions, visitors to Calgary in 1913 could not help but be impressed with the many significant buildings in the business centre. While each made a contribution to the emerging metropolitan environment, a number stood out as noteworthy examples of commercial and architectural achievement.

One of the most prominent structures erected in this period was the Grain Exchange Building. Owned by William Roper Hull, a successful and respected promoter of agriculture in southern Alberta, it became the headquarters of Calgary's nascent grain marketing, handling and investment industry. The Grain Exchange Building owned its existence primarily to the fact that Calgary was situated in the midst of productive agricultural land, and to the fact that certain local entrepreneurs anxiously sought to rival Winnipeg's control of agricultural marketing in western Canada. During autumn 1908, the finest crop in the province's history was harvested. That year the district between High River and Claresholm held the CPR's record for the largest grain shipment, with 2.4 million bushels being transported to eastern markets.[7] This movement of enormous quantities of grain to the east, together with the maintenance of attractive prices, prompted local businessmen and members of the Calgary Board of Trade to take steps toward establishing a grain exchange, in the hopes of deflecting some of the region's extensive prosperity to the city.[8] Interest was high among investors and entrepreneurs, as the proposed Panama Canal route meant that grain would eventually be shipped to west coast ports, and that new grain handling and marketing facilities would be required. It was thought that Calgary was strategically located and would thus figure largely in future developments. Accordingly, a grain exchange was founded in August 1909, with sixty members.[9] William Roper Hull, an avid supporter of the venture, subsequently agreed to let the organization use a portion of his new building,[10] located at the corner of Ninth Avenue and First Street West.

Grain Exchange Building, Calgary, 1910

The Grain Exchange Building was designed by the Calgary architectural firm of Hodgson and Bates.[11] It was started in 1908 and was almost finished by the end of the next year, but was not actually occupied until early in 1910.[12]

Archibald and Company of Winnipeg and Calgary were the contractors for the project, variously estimated at between $100,000 and $150,000.[13] The building was essentially classical in style; among its many features was a heavy cornice with dentils, a parapet and decorative balustrade. In the main façade which faced First Street West, Ionic pilasters rose from the fourth storey to the cornice level, dividing the top section of the building into five equal bays.[14] The sandstone was smooth-dressed in this panel, in contrast to the rough, rock-faced stone which was used in the rest of the building. At ground level, heraldic mouldings were carved on top of the main piers, and a scrolled name plate was positioned above the main entrance. This high level of craftsmanship added greatly to the appeal of the building, and helped it to become a noted landmark in the downtown district.

Upon its completion, the Grain Exchange Building became one of the busiest and most celebrated commercial blocks in the city. In 1908, only two firms were in the grain business in Calgary; by 1913, that number had grown to over forty.[15] Many of the grain companies, brokers and elevator companies drawn to the city by the sudden blossoming of the grain trade took up office space in this new and highly desirable location (see Appendix B). The Grain Exchange thus quickly became a well-known site in the emerging skyline, and a symbol of Calgary's rising importance as an agricultural marketing centre.

The erection of the Grain Exchange Building was an important event not only in terms of Calgary's commercial expansion, but also in terms of architectural development in the city. Built with an internal reinforced concrete frame devised only a few years before in the mid-western United States by Albert Kahn,[16] it represented the first truly modern business block in Calgary.[17] Sandstone, a traditional material in Calgary's commercial buildings for years, was used solely as a decorative veneer in the structure. The Grain Exchange Building was a distinctly advanced design, a true credit to the city's modernity. Erected at a time when concrete construction was still a novelty throughout North America and Great Britain,[18] it demonstrated that Calgary had entered the mainstream of modern building technology and architectural fashion. Moreover, the building indicated that local entrepreneurs were ardent connoisseurs of progress and played a significant role in creating a modern, aggressive business atmosphere in the city.

From 1910 onwards, commercial buildings of six or more storeys became more numerous in Calgary's central business district for several reasons. First, business growth in the city was a constant factor on account of the agricultural development of the region, and opportunities it generated for profitable investment and the phenomenal expansion of the city. The accelerating demand for prime office, retail and wholesale space necessitated the construction of buildings of grand dimensions. Second, real estate prices were ever on the increase, especially in the downtown core. Between 1882 and 1912, property values on Eighth Avenue jumped 1,000 percent,[19] while adjacent land rose in a similarly dramatic fashion. As a result, building costs skyrocketed: a denser arrangement of business facilities was clearly called for. Third, new building materials and construction techniques that were currently being utilized in Chicago, New York, and eastern Canadian cities became available in Calgary. With the influx of a large number of eastern Canadian and British-trained architects and engineers, and the implementation of industrially prefabricated materials in building construction, new solutions to space shortages and economic exigencies were made possible. Multi-storeyed buildings with reinforced concrete and rivetted steel frames, and curtain walls of glass, terra cotta, stone or brickwork thus soon took precedence over smaller, solid masonry structures in Calgary's business centre. Fourth, the adoption of new and progressive building regulations underscored the trend toward tall and fully modern building designs. With the general increase in the assessed value of all buildings in the downtown core, city officials became increasingly rigorous in imposing fire limits and prescribing building standards which guaranteed the safety of property.[20] In 1911, the type of buildings that were allowed to be erected in the first class fire limit in the city centre had to be "equal in structure and material to those of any of the largest cities in Canada."[21] By 1912, Calgary was renowned for having the most advanced building code, as well as some of the most impressive commercial buildings in western Canada.[22]

Lougheed Building, Calgary, 1912

Two of the largest structures built in the city during those years were the Beveridge, Travis and Alberta Loan and Investment Company Block and the Lougheed Building. Both massive edifices were erected in 1911 and 1912 by prominent real estate investors anxious to capitalize on the high demand for prime office and retail space.[23] The Beveridge Block was five storeys in height and had a frontage of 175 feet on Seventh Avenue and 135 feet on First Street East.[24] Opened in February of 1912, the $500,000 structure initially housed various small businesses including Enterprise Electric, Riley and McCormick, and numerous real estate and mortgage companies.[25] Several blocks to the west was the larger and more expensive Lougheed Building. Six storeys in height, it measured 200 feet along Sixth Avenue and 130 feet along First Street West. It cost between $600,000 and $700,000, and when finished in autumn 1912 became the most unique multi-purpose commercial building in the city. As well as accommodating fifteen retail stores and the Sherman Grand Theatre in the ground floor, and office space for assorted companies and professionals in the second, third and fourth storeys, it was divided into two and three-room residential suites in the fifth and sixth storeys[26] (see Appendix B).

Like most other large business buildings erected in the city at the height of the boom period, both the Beveridge Block and the Lougheed Building were modern architectural designs with traditional masonry façades and classical features. But unlike many other structures, they were situated on huge tracts of land and were thus massive and remarkably horizontal in appearance. As real estate values continued to soar, however, the height of many office buildings began to exceed their horizontal dimensions. By October 1912, for example, commercial sites on Eighth Avenue were worth as much as $4,000 per front foot.[27] This fact, together with the proliferation of commercial establishments and the centralization of business administration in downtown Calgary exerted considerable pressure of developers and speculators for more intensive land use and, consequently, the erection of more tall buildings. As well, it became apparent that skyscrapers, as they became known, were not only functionally but aesthetically suited to the requirements of the city's most active businessmen, who were fascinated and even obsessed with material progress, development and achievement.[28]

One of the earliest and most elegant skyscrapers erected in the city at this time was the P. Burns Building. Located on the corner of Eighth Avenue and Second Street East, it was an impressive structure owned by Patrick Burns, one of the city's most illustrious millionaires. Burns was not only a

ranching tycoon and proprietor of the largest food
processing and distributing industry in western Canada,
but he was also a noted investor in local property, and a
firm believer in the city's destiny as a commercial and
manufacturing centre.[29] He apparently bought the property
and planned the erection of the structure known as the
Burns Building as early as summer 1909.[30] But because of
financial stringencies and perhaps anticipated appreciation
of land, he decided instead to pour his money into his
ranching and meat packing operations.[31] Burns thus
delayed construction of his building for some time.
Excavation of the site did not begin until autumn 1911,
while actual construction work was not commenced until
the following April.[32] By March 1913, the building was
ready for tenants to move in[33].

The Burns Building, Calgary, c. 1913

The Burns Building was yet another design by architects
Hodgson, Bates and Beattie.[34] It was six storeys in height
and was constructed with the Kahn system of reinforced

concrete, a fireproof structural feature well-proven with the firm in Calgary. Highly fashionable in appearance, it was decorated with white terra cotta panels on the north, south and east elevations, and styled in an Edwardian classical manner, with engaged pilasters, an entablature above the second storey, a prominent cornice with dentils, and an inscribed frieze band.[35] Lions' heads and other highly ornamental mouldings sculptured in the surface of the terra cotta helped relieve the bareness of the building's tall, rectangular form. Another interesting feature was the large wrought iron and glass canopy which extended around the east and north sides, and which reduced the scale of the building to passers-by. Inside, white and green Italian marble was used to decorate the main stairway and corridors.[36] Comfort and convenience were also emphasized: in addition to modern steam heating, ventilation and electrical appliances in the building, natural gas was piped into each office for lighting purposes.[37]

Pat Burns paid approximately $350,000 for his new office showpiece,[38] described by the *Herald* as "Calgary's finest business block."[39] But aside from using the ground floor for a meat market, the P. Burns Company had no direct association with the new facility, preferring instead to maintain its head offices in a considerably humbler building in east Calgary[40] and to lease out the nearly thirty-five thousand square feet of office space at lucrative rates to various companies which initially included Calgary Power, Alberta Investment and Insurance Brokers, Rocky Mountain Cement, American Sewer Pipe, and various doctors, dentists, lawyers, realtors, insurance agents and accountants.[41]

Shortly before construction of the Burns Building was started, the *Herald* announced that another handsome office building was planned for the corner of Eighth Avenue and Second Street West.[42] The Canada Life Assurance Building was a striking design, and represented a sophisticated departure from the plain, box-like business blocks in the downtown area. Like the Burns Building it was six storeys in height and clad in beautifully worked white terra cotta. Brown and Vallance of Montreal were the

Canada Life Building, Calgary, 1912

architects of the structure,[43] and Fysche, McNeil, Martin
and Trainer were the general contractors.[44] The Canada
Life Building was a thoroughly modern work of
architecture. Steel and concrete were the principal
components of the internal frame, while on the exterior
the building took on a smooth, streamlined shape which
expressed the engineering potentialities of metal under
stress and other highly plastic building materials which
were utilized in its construction. Also of note were the tall
round-arched bays in each façade which extended from
the second to the sixth storey; and in which numerous

Herald Building, Calgary, c. 1913

large windows were set. These perpendicular divisions
gave the building a remarkable soaring quality. The profuse
decoration of each elevation with ornamental mouldings,
including the provincial emblem, further enhanced the
building's attractiveness. The Canada Life Building was the
most consistent example of the Chicago School of modern
architecture in the city. In many respects, it was not unlike
Louis Sullivan's Guaranteed Trust Building in Buffalo, New
York, in its strong vertical emphasis, subordination of
design to new building materials and commercial function,
and its dramatization of the building's engineered form

with lavish ornamentation.[45] When it was opened in October 1913,[46] the Canada Life Building became an ideal business address for the leading insurance companies, financial brokers, lawyers, accountants and other professionals prominent in the metropolitan business community (see Appendix B). As well as being one of the most singular buildings in Calgary, it further signalled the westward expansion of Calgary's central business district, a movement that was temporarily interrupted by the outbreak of war in Europe one year later.

Skyscraper construction during the boom years reached its zenith with the completion of the ten-storey Herald Building late in 1913. Located on the corner of Seventh Avenue and First Street West, next to the Lougheed Building, it was a towering structure, elegant in proportion and pleasing in overall design. The new building provided vastly improved facilities for the operation of the *Calgary Daily Herald* newspaper. Moreover, it was the tallest and most expensive office building in the city, and was hailed as the finest commercial edifice between Winnipeg and the coast.[47]

Plans for the magnificent building were announced in March 1912.[48] By June, the preliminary task of demolishing the old First Baptist Church which occupied the site was under way.[49] The contract for the project, reportedly worth $750,000, was subsequently awarded to Fysche, McNeil, Martin and Trainer on July 31, with the stipulation that the building would be finished by August 1, 1913.[50] Work proceeded rapidly throughout the winter months and during the following summer the *Herald* began to advertise first class office space in the facility for rent.[31] In November, Calgary's most prestigious modern office building was ready for occupancy,[52] although the *Herald* did not relocate to its new home until December 13.[53]

The Herald Building was another work by the architectural firm of Brown and Vallance of Montréal. Organized on an essentially square plan, it measured one hundred feet along Seventh Avenue and ninety feet along First Street West.[55] Great care was taken by all involved to ensure that it was "as modern as modern architecture and construction [could] make."[56] Like other skyscrapers in the city, it was of fireproof design, with a reinforced concrete and steel frame, and was faced with brown kitanning brick and white ornamental terra cotta.[57] All the materials used in the structure were tested beforehand to ensure they met the standards of the Canadian Society of Engineers.[58] Inside, the most up-to-date building services and tasteful fittings were incorporated to make it the most sought-after business location in the city.

As well s being the largest skyscraper in the city, the Herald Building was also the most visually interesting commercial structure. The first two storeys were particularly noteworthy, with their fine sculptured details. On the ground floor, seven tall, rounded arches along the main façades gave the building a rhythmic sense to those who walked or drove by. Above the arches, superbly crafted ceramic figurines in the shape of caricatured newspaper personalities, expressive faces and Gothic-inspired animal gargoyles added greatly to the unusual charm of the building.[59] Separating the upper vertical portion of the structure from the lower level was a traceried moulding which extended horizontally above the second storey. As in the Canada Life Building, each facade was divided into numerous perpendicular bays which rose from the third storey and terminated in round headed windows in the eighth storey. Decorative shields moulded in white terra cotta were placed just above those bays. The top portion of the building repeated the tall arches and sculptural detail of the bottom storeys, thereby giving the building a sense of balance and coherence. Crowning the structure was a heavy brick parapet with ribs and decorative terra cotta battlements. In terms of derivative architectural style, the Herald Building followed the Chicago School of tall building design with its emphasis on modern structural systems, building services and innovative exterior decoration. Gothic qualities were strongly expressed in the verticality of the structure and in the various carved motifs in both the lower and upper storeys,[60] making it one of a kind in the city, and perhaps in the west.

The illustrious Herald Building was the first skyscraper to

reach beyond the six-storey level in the city. More important, though, it provided accommodation for various administrative offices, professional corporations, doctors, lawyers, realtors, advertising companies and financial organizations. And since its opening conveniently coincided with the beginnings of the oil bonanza in the Turner Valley,[61] it also became one of the choice business addresses for the innumerable oil companies, investment syndicates, geologists, and service industries that flooded into the city in search of overnight fortunes (see Appendix B).

Office buildings were not the only tall commercial structures erected in the city at the height of the boom period. Both the Hudson's Bay Company store and the Canadian Pacific Railway's Palliser Hotel were also constructed with the latest in concrete and steel technology, and represented substantial investments in response to heightened opportunities to do profitable business in Calgary. With the tremendous population explosion and the relatively high level of prosperity in the city, the time was right for a significant expansion in the local retail trade. In an effort to obtain the lion's share of this business, the Hudson's Bay Company responded by erecting the largest retail emporium in the city. Similarly, an increase in the number of regional, national and international travellers in the city on both business and pleasure excursions necessitated the construction of an elaborate form of housing. One of the largest landowners in Calgary and unmistakably the prime mover of economic development in the west, the CPR eagerly took up the challenge and built a dignified hotel that was truly a credit to the community and, at the same time, a monument to its own commerical power and prestige.

Built between 1911 and 1913, the new Hudson's Bay Company store was the most renowned facility in Calgary, and in the official words of *The Beaver,* a Company publication, "unsurpassed by any departmental store on the continent."[62] It represented the first modern store erected under the Company's new expansion programme, and also indicated a changed perception of Calgary's commercial importance.[63] Company officials recognized that with the growth of the western Canadian economy, Calgary had an assured future as a regional centre. The mammoth store that was subsequently erected on the corner of Seventh Avenue and First Street West was worthy of a city of a million people.[64] It thus signified the confidence of Canada's oldest commercial establishment in the continued growth of Calgary.

Hudson's Bay Company store, Calgary

This majestic building was designed by Burke, Horwood and White of Toronto.[65] Six storeys in height with foundations capable of supporting four additional floors and built entirely of structural steel, concrete and brick, it was a model of modern retail architecture.[66] According to the *Herald*, it looked more like a museum than a store.[67] Cream glaze terra cotta decorated the entire frontage, giving it a luxurious appearance.[68] This effect was further enhanced by the use of copper window frames and granite footings in the ground storey, and by the expression of Edwardian classical details, such as engaged pilasters between the second and fifth storeys, a lightly detailed cornice and elegant balustrade along the top level. Elaborate mouldings, such as the company's coat of arms on the corner piers, also added to the building's opulent character.

Inside the palatial structure, 222,952 square feet of floor space[69] were organized into forty retail departments, storage facilities, offices and building maintenance rooms. Every known device for fire protection and customer comfort was adopted.[70] In addition to having the "best ventilation system known to modern science," the building had a stationary vacuum cleaner system, a pneumatic tube delivery system, ten Otis Fenson elevators, its own independent power generating plant and an artesian well in the basement.[71] The store provided an extraordinary environment where patrons could get a good taste of big city elegance. Rich carpets bearing the Company crest, fittings of brass and mahogany, palm trees, flowers and high quality merchandise imported from around the world created an atmosphere conducive to graceful shopping.[72] Other conveniences included a nursery, women's rest room, men's smoking lounge, circulating library, post office, telegraphic station and a playground for children on the roof.[73] Perhaps the highlight of the interior was the spacious dining room on the sixth floor which offered Calgarians and visitors alike the utmost in elegant decor. Finished in Elizabethan style, with oak panelling, period furniture, rich draperies and stained glass, it commemorated the approximate period in history during which the Hudson's Bay Company Charter was granted.[74]

Plans to build the new store were known as early as March 7, 1911, when Senator James Lougheed sold the site to the Hudson's Bay Company.[75] Excavation was completed by October of that year, but for reasons that are not clear, construction did not commence until March 22, 1912.[76] The Carter, Halls and Aldinger Company were awarded the contract for the building, which cost $2.5 million in total to erect.[77] By the middle of July 1912, the steel superstructure was almost halfway up. A year later, the building was practically finished, and on August 18, 1913, it was officially opened to the public amidst great pomp and ceremony.[78] According to the *Albertan*, the great store compared favourably with Harrod's of London, England,[74] and illustrated very eloquently the city's sudden coming of age.

Next to the Hudsons' Bay Company store, the Palliser Hotel was the most expensive commercial building erected in Calgary during the boom years. Built at a cost of $1.5 million,[80] it offered a level of luxury and refinement to tourists, businessmen and local residents that was unparalleled in the region. At the same time, the adoption of up-to-date architectural features made it one of the safest and most modern structures in the city.

Plans for the new CPR hotel were announced in January 1911 following negotiations with city officials.[81] Decision makers at City Hall apparently agreed to free the company from the burden of property taxes, providing that it paid $4,000 per year and undertook half of the costs of paving Ninth Avenue from First Street West to First Street East, as well as one-quarter of the cost of paving the road to Fifth Street East.[82] Ground was broken at the building site on September 23, and with the installation of a steam heating unit, concrete for the foundation was mixed and poured throughout the winter.[83] By July 1912, the erection of the structural steel frame was proceeding rapidly.[84] But due to inevitable lags in construction, the facility was not ready for business until early in 1914, several months after the anticipated completion date.[85]

The Palliser Hotel was designed by Montréal architects E. and W.S. Maxwell.[86] It was an imposing edifice, eight storeys high, and built with an internal structural system of concrete and steel that was capable of supporting an additional five storeys.[87] Like many other tall buildings in the city, it combined traditional styling with new materials and construction techniques. It was fashioned in the classical spirit of architecture[88] with various refined details moulded in the smooth-dressed concrete. Organized on a symmetrical, E-shaped plan with three individual towers, it featured numerous large, round-headed windows with radiating voissoirs in the first storey, two Ionic colonnades separated by the main entranceway in the north facade, string courses above the first and second storeys and a well-defined cornice above the eighth storey. Also planned but not built was a French-styled mansard roof.[89]

146

Palliser Hotel, Calgary

The interior of the Palliser Hotel was likewise tastefully appointed. Marble floors, apple-green rugs and tapestries hanging from the walls in the main lobby helped to create a rich, sophisticated atmosphere that was carried throughout the rest of the building in the dining room, palm court, ball room and in the 350 suites in the upper floors.[90]

The immense Palliser Hotel was built in the European tradition of luxury hotels, exemplified by the Ritz in London, which was completed in 1906.[91] Acclaimed as the finest hotel between Vancouver and Winnipeg, it was primarily designed to provide specialized accommodation for regional, national and even international clientele—wholesale buyers and sellers, investors, administrators and recreational travellers—who visited the city either regularly or occasionally. The Palliser Hotel swiftly became a symbol of metropolitan affluence and the conspicuous consumption of the privileged classes in Calgary. As one of the most dominant architectural forms in the urban skyline, it was also a highly visible reminder to all of the importance of the Canadian Pacific Railway to Calgary's past development and hopes for the future.

In summary, Calgary's emergence as an aggressive commercial centre prior to World War I was highly evident in the buildings that were erected in the business district.These structures not only provided ample space for a growing number of corporations, financial institutions, professional services and small businesses, but also demonstrated that Calgary was indeed a counterpart of other large commercial centres such as Winnipeg, Toronto and Montréal in economic function and appearance. Most were traditional in appearance, suggesting perhaps an inclination toward Edwardian classical fashions, while others such as the Canada Life Building and the Herald Building were more remarkable, indicating that the design ideals of the Chicago School of architecture were gaining sway. More important than external styling, though, these tall, substantial buildings were all products of the latest in technological innovations fundamental to skyscraper construction, and were as modern as could be found in Canada.

The advantages of modern commercial building construction were well publicized in Calgary in these years. As well as representing a more economical use of expensive land in the business centre and providing a maximum of internal comfort, convenience and safety to occupants, these buildings could be erected more efficiently. The MacLean Building, for example, a six-storey office structure which was constructed with 4,000 yards of concrete, 2,000 tons of steel, 300 tons of stone and over 750,000 bricks, was erected in the space of five months and two days.[92] The many substantial commercial edifices that were subsequently built in Calgary were not only testimony to the affluence but also to the technologically progressive outlook and opportunistic attitude of the city's business leaders.

# Small Commercial Buildings and Industrial Structures

Because of increased economic pressure on land at the peak of the boom, few small-time investors could afford to erect commercial buildings of less than four storeys in the central business district. Escalating real estate values necessitated the construction of progressively taller buildings with large areas of leasable floor space in order for even wealthy entrepreneurs to make a profitable return on their investments. But with the phenomenal increase in Calgary's residential population, new markets for goods and services were created in outlying areas. Opportunities flourished for all kinds of merchants, small businessmen, tradesmen and professionals, especially in the densely populated suburbs. This pattern of commercial expansion was further underscored by the extension of electric street railway lines along major transportation routes. By 1912, there were innumerable small commercial buildings along Tenth Street Northwest, Ninth Avenue East, Seventeenth Avenue West and Fourth Street West. Most of these structures were between one and three storeys high, and were built on concrete foundations with wooden frames and red brick exterior walls.[93]

Of the several districts in which the electric street car system operated, Hillhurst had the best service outside of the downtown area.[94] This not only encouraged more people to live nearby, but also increased traffic along Tenth Street and Boulevard Northwest, thereby attracting considerable commercial development in the vicinity. Among the many businesses located there by 1912 were: several grocery stores, meat markets, confectioneries, cafés, men's and womens' wear stores, hardware dealers, barber shops, pool halls, shoe repair shops, doctors' offices, assorted tradesmen's shops, and numerous professional and financial agencies.[95] Several of the buildings at the corner, including the Ross, Kerr and Carscallen blocks, also had small apartments in their upper storeys..[96] Like other small business buildings across the city, the structures at the Hillhurst intersection were remarkably similar in appearance. Most were two storeys high and starkly classical in design, with red brick exteriors, pressed metal cornices, plain rectangular windows and some sandstone trim. All were cheaply built: the new Ross Block, which provided space for a bowling alley, seven stores, a large hall and a few apartments, cost a mere $60,000 to erect in 1911,[97] a marked contrast to the extravagant prices for buildings in the downtown area.

Business block, Hillhurst area, Calgary

Industrial growth was also a significant aspect of Calgary's economic expansion during this period. In 1905, there were only a few manufacturing plants in the city, most of which were directly related to agriculture and the local building concerns.[98] By 1913, Calgary had taken its place as one of the most prominent manufacturing centres on the Canadian plains. That year, a total of four thousand workers were employed in local industries which numbered approximately sixty.[99]

Of these industries, the most impressive and doubtless the most beneficial to the city's overall growth was the Canadian Pacific Railway's locomotive and car repair shops. Located southeast of the city limits at a site appropriately named after CPR Vice-president I.E. Ogden,[100] the operation was reported to be one of the biggest ever undertaken by the railway, and among the largest and most modern shops on the continent.[101] It included twenty separate buildings on 120 acres,[102] and initially gave employment to three thousand men, with prospects for another two thousand.[103] The *Albertan* estimated that the construction of the enormous complex would bring at least ten thousand more people to the city, and a deluge of further investment in commercial and residential development.[104]

CPR shops, Ogden, Alberta

The decision of the CPR to erect its enormous shops at Ogden was announced by the *Herald* on December 15, 1911.[105] Following the completion of survey work, ground was broken at the site on April 1, 1912, and construction commenced nearly two weeks later.[106] At the outset, close to three hundred men were involved in building activities,[107] but this number swelled to almost eleven hundred by July.[108] Construction proved difficult, however, on account of the sheer magnitude of the project, its remote location[109] and a shortage of labour in the city.[110] Workers apparently had to be transported back and forth from Calgary on an electric street railway line that had been specially built by the city upon request of the CPR.[111] Some workers also found lodging in the hotels and numerous dwellings that were erected almost overnight in the nearby subdivision of Ceepeear.[112] Despite these problems, remarkable progress was made in a short while. By March 17, 1913, all of the principal shops at the site were in operation.[113]

The gigantic industrial facility, worth an estimated $2.5 million,[114] was designed by Westinghouse, Church, Kerr and Company, Consulting and Constructing Engineers of New York and Montréal.[115] Among the most important buildings on the site were the locomotive shop, foundry, wheel shop, planing mill and coach repair and paint shop. Inside, blast furnaces, ten-ton travelling cranes, hoists, and other heavy machines for crushing, drilling and cutting metal could be seen, as well as numerous locomotives, boxcars and passenger cars in various stages of repair.[116] Most of these main buildings were constructed with steel frames and a bewildering multiplicity of roof trusses, concrete foundations and ceramic tile-backed masonry and concrete walls.[117] The locomotive shop, the largest structure within the complex, alone covered six acres and provided stalls and pits for repairing up to thirty-five engines at one time.[118] All machine tools at the site were electrically powered, and all building services, including the ducts for the indirect fan heating system and water pipes for the fire-fighting system, were carried underground to ensure safety and a maximum of internal space.[119]

Next only to the Angus shops in Montréal in size and importance to the CPR,[120] the Ogden shops were erected for the purpose of overhauling the entire western rolling stock of the railway once a year.[121] In spite of the fact that other western Canadian centres had offered free sites, cheap electrical power and other concessions that were even greater than those offered by local officials, Calgary was chosen as the site of the shops on account of its strategic situation on the edge of both the prairies and the mountain region.[122] In building their repair complex at Ogden, the CPR once again confirmed the city's role as the greatest railway hub in the west and its potential as a large-scale centre of industrial development.

Another building of similar importance and construction

was the new P. Burns Company meat packing plant, located in East Calgary. On January 12, 1913, fire destroyed the old abattoir, long considered an institution in western Canada.[123] Damage was estimated at nearly $2 million, including nearly $1 million worth of stock.[124] Not to be outdone by natural catastrophe, Burns announced plans almost immediately to rebuild the facility on even grander proportions,[125] and work was suddenly under way. By the middle of November of that same year, it was finished.[126] The new, thoroughly fireproof plant was designed by Gardner and Lindberg, engineers and architects from Chicago, and erected by L.R. Burn, a Calgary contractor.[127] It was five storeys high, with a total floor space of 148,000 square feet[128] which was divided into special areas for slaughtering, butchering and storing animal carcasses. Altogether, 12,000 barrels of cement, 425 tons of steel and 1.4 million bricks were used in its construction.[129] When completed, the *Herald* noted that it was the largest building of its class in the west.[130] The new industrial complex clearly indicated Burns's willingness to overlook financial losses in an effort to develop the city's latent industrial potential.

The extensive CPR shops, the new Burns plant and other manufacturing establishments, such as the enormous reinforced concrete elevator for the Canada Malting Company,[131] were built entirely in response to Calgary's favoured position as a transportation centre, locus of agricultural production and steady source of labour. They were all utilitarian buildings constructed with machine-made materials and modern ingenuity, and they reflected their economic function as shelters for industrial activities. Industries represented long-term investment in the city, and since profitable production was to a great degree predicated upon the modernity and efficiency of operations, considerable attention was given to the internal organization of buildings and the adoption of the most up-to-date equipment available. Hence, unlike small commercial structures which were generally simple in design and inexpensive in construction, these huge facilities incorporated the latest in engineering expertise, building technology and devices for building safety and comfort.

Despite dismal economic conditions just prior to World War I, both residents and visitors to Calgary could not help but be impressed with the city's meteoric rise. The many new office blocks, stores, hotels, manufacturing plants and other structures that were erected in the boom years represented a considerable capital investment in the city's future. In addition, they provided conspicuous evidence of Calgary's economic dominance over a vast hinterland and proof of its status as a full-fledged metropolis.

Halfway through 1909, the *Herald* boastfully predicted that as the value of Eighth Avenue and adjacent frontages climbed, storeys would begin to pile on top of one another.[132] This prophecy was soon fulfilled: within a short time it was apparent that Calgary's chief business buildings had passed the two-storey stage and were stretching beyond the six to the ten-storey stage. These immense structures were fireproof, durable and could be erected more quickly than conventional masonry buildings. Furthermore, they offered distinct financial advantages to owners and investors. Tall steel and concrete buildings had a greater load-bearing capacity, and thus opened up a maximum of floor space serviced with the latest mechanical utilities which could be rented out at profitable prices. This fact more than compensated for escalating land values in the downtown area. Aside from erecting structures that were principally good investments, local entrepreneurs and national corporate executives also commissioned the construction of fully modern designs to advertise the wealth, modern outlook and faith of their organizations in the city's prosperous destiny. Thus, as well as having obvious commercial functions, these buildings were also symbolic of the triumph of capitalism in creating yet another vibrant metropolitan community where, only forty years before, had been vast open prairie.

The introduction of new, industrially produced materials, and the application of novel construction methods and architectural styles first developed in the midwestern United States proved crucial to this transformation of the local economy and the urban landscape. With the increased use of prefabricated concrete slabs and posts, steel beams, terra cotta panels, hollow ceramic tiles, dry pressed brick, and mechanical building services, and the rapid assembly rather than hand-crafted construction of buildings, it was evident that Calgary had entered what Lewis Mumford describes as the machine age of modern architecture.[133] Eastern Canadian or American architects and engineers became the logical choice of local businessmen and national companies who wished to erect fully modern commercial and industrial buildings, since their technical knowledge was based on years of practice with progressive designs. At the same time, however, local architects were becoming more adept in their work. But in spite of a general advancement in building construction in the city, there were a few problems. The collapse of the Bruner Building while being erected in 1911[134] illustrated the consequences of inexperience with new materials and a hectic pace of construction. Also, an excessive demand for cement and brick resulted in periodic shortages during 1910 and 1911, which had the effect of slowing construction to an extent.[135] These difficulties were minor, however, and were to be expected in a period of frantic construction activity.

## Notes

[1] *Herald,* January 20, 1909.

[2] *Herald,* June 26, 1909: *Construction* 3, no. 2 (December 1909): p. 112; MacRae, *History of the Province of Alberta,* vol. 2, p. 636.

[3] The Bailey brothers and A.J. Samis were noted investors in local real estate. See H.L. Macleod, "Properties, Investors and Taxes," Appendices A and F.

[4] *Albertan,* February 28, 1911.

[5] *Albertan,* January 4, 1912.

[6] *Henderson's Directory,* 1913, p. 147.

[7] *News Telegram,* January 18, 1909.

[8] *Ibid.: Albertan,* January 16, 1909.

[9] *Albertan,* February 28, 1913.

[10]*News Telegram*, January 16, 1909.

[11]GAI, W.S. Bates Papers.

[12]*Albertan*, February 28, 1910.

[13]*Herald*, October 12, 1912. An early estimate of $100,000 was reported by the *Herald* on April 1, 1909, and on June 26, 1909, the newspaper noted the cost at $125,000.

[14]See G.P. Utas, "Calgary Architecture," pp. 54-55.

[15]*Albertan*, February 28, 1913.

[16]MacRae, *History of the Province of Alberta*, vol. 1, pp. 581-583. City of Calgary, PHSE, vol. 2, category 8, file 133.

[17]See Carl W. Condit, *American Building* (Chicago: University of Chicago Press, 1968), pp. 241-242.

[18]See *News Telegram*, January 6, 1909.

[19]*News Telegram*, January 11, 1913.

[20]*Albertan*, February 28, 1911.

[21]*Ibid.*

[22]*Albertan*, February 28, 1913.

[23]For details on other real estate holdings of the Beveridge brothers, Judge Travis and Sir James Lougheed, see H.L. Macleod, "Properties, Investors and Taxes," Appendices A to F.

[24]*News Telegram*, February 17, 1912. In actuality, the structure consisted of three buildings which were owned by separate parties, but were combined in one design by architects Hodgson, Bates and Beattie.

[25]*Ibid.*

[26]*Herald*, September 14, 21, 28, October 5, 16, 1912. According to *Construction* 6, no. 12 (October 1913), pp. 373-374, the building was designed by R. Wardrop.

[27]*Herald*, October 12, 1912.

[28]See Lewis Mumford, *Roots of Contemporary American Architecture* (New York: Reinhold Publishing Corporation, 1952; reprint ed., Dover Publications, 1972), pp. 20-23.

[29]See A.F. Sproule, "The Role of Patrick Burns in the Development of Western Canada" (Unpublished Master's thesis, University of Alberta, 1962) for a thorough discussion of Burns's entrepreneurial accomplishments.

[30]*Herald*, August 14, 1909.

[31]A.F. Sproule, "Patrick Burns," pp. 141-142.

[32]*Herald*, February 1, 1913.

[33]*Ibid.*

[34]*Herald*, July 18, 1912.

[35]GAI, W.S. Bates Papers, Original Plans of the Burns Building.

[36]*Herald*, February 1, 1913.

[37]*Ibid.*

[38]*Construction* 6, no. 12 (October 1913): p. 373.

[39]*Herald*, February 1, 1913.

[40]*Henderson's Directory*, 1913, advertisement.

[41]*Ibid.*

[42]*Herald*, March 10, 1912.

[43]*Ibid.*

[44]*The 100,000 Manufacturing, Building and Wholesale Book Edition* (Calgary: *Morning Albertan*, 1914), p. 56.

[45]City of Calgary, PHSE, vol. 2, category 46, file 8; G.P. Utas, "Calgary Architecture," pp. 86-87; Wayne Andrews, *Architecture, Ambition and Americans—A Social History of American Architecture* (New York: The Free Press, 1964), pp. 212, 219, 228.

[46]*Herald*, October 11, 1913.

[47]*Herald*, July 31, 1912.

[48]*Herald*, March 18, 1912.

[49]*Herald*, June 8, 1912.

[50]*Herald*, July 31, 1912.

[51]For examples, see *Herald*, July 28, 29, 31, 1913.

[52]*Herald*, October 18, 1913.

[53]*Herald*, December 13, 1913.

[54]*Herald*, July 31, 1912.

[55]*Ibid.*

[56]*Herald*, June 8, 1912. Author's brackets.

[57]*Herald*, July 31, 1912.

[58]*Ibid.*

[59]These figures were designed by Royal Doulton in England, and were the property of the Southam family, owners of the building. Although the Herald Building was demolished in 1971 to make way for the Len Werry Building, some of these figures were salvaged and are on display in the Garden Terrace of the Calgary Convention Centre, and also at The University of Calgary, Science B Building entrance.

[60]See G.P. Utas, "Calgary Architecture," pp. 84-85.

[61]*Herald*, October 10, 1913.

[62]J. Brown, "Calgary—the City of the Foothills," *The Beaver* 2, no. 7 (April 1922): p. 3.

[63]*Ibid.*

[64]*Ibid.*

[65]*Herald*, April 13, 1912.

[66]J. Brown, "Calgary," p. 3; *Herald*, March 22, 1912.

[67]*Herald*, April 13, 1912.

[68]*Construction* 6, no. 12 (October 1913): p. 374.

[69]J. Brown, "Calgary," pp. 2-4. The floor dimensions for the store were 130 feet by 245 feet; hence the area cited must include the basement and the playground on the roof as floor space.

[70]*Herald*, April 13, 1912.

[71]*Albertan*, August 9, 1913.

[72]*Ibid.*

[73]*Ibid.*

[74]See *Herald,* August 19, 1913.

[75]*Albertan,* March 7, 1911.

[76]*Herald,* March 22, 1912.

[77]J. Brown, "Calgary," p. 3.

[78]*Herald,* July 16, 1912, August 19, 1913.

[79]*Albertan,* August 9, 1913.

[80]*Herald,* October 12, 1912.

[81]*Albertan,* January 17, 1911.

[82]*Ibid.*

[83]*Herald,* November 3, 1911.

[84]*News Telegram,* January 18, 1913.

[85]*Ibid.*

[86]*Construction* 6, no. 12 (October 1913): p. 373.

[87]*Albertan,* May 16, 1911; see City of Calgary, PHSE, vol. 3, category 13, file 208.

[88]*Architecture: Some Beautiful Effects Obtained by Architects and Master Painters.* According to a promotional pamphlet, (Montréal: Sherwin Williams Paints, 1914), the hotel was designed in the classical style from in the period of Louis XVI.

[89]See *Henderson's Directory,* 1913, p. 143 for sketch; also see *News Telegram,* January 3, 1913.

[90]GAI, Photo Archives.

[91]Service, *Edwardian Architecture,* p. 162.

[92]*News Telegram,* February 2, 1912.

[93]See City of Calgary, PHSE, vol. 3, category 10, *passim,* for examples.

[94]*Herald,* November 3, 1911.

[95]*Henderson's Directory,* 1912.

[96]*Ibid.*

[97]*Herald*, May 27, 1911.

[98]M.L. Foran, *Calgary an Illustrated History*, p. 70; also see Paul Voisey, "In Search of Wealth and Status," in *Frontier Calgary*, ed. Rasporich and Klassen, p. 224.

[99]*Calgary Board of Trade Annual Report*, 1913, President's Address. Also *Census of Canada*, 1911, vol. 3, table 9, p. 210.

[100]See *Strathmore Standard*, April 8, 1912, for details on the career of I.E. Ogden, GAI, Newspaper Clippings File.

[101]*Albertan*, February 28, 1912.

[102]According to the *Albertan*, February 28, 1913, the CPR acquired an additional 410 acres which were reserved for future expansion.

[103]*Ibid.*

[104]*Ibid. Herald*, May 4, 1912.

[105]*Herald*, December 15, 1911.

[106]*Herald*, April 17, 1912.

[107]*Herald*, May 4, 1912.

[108]*Herald*, August 3, 1912.

[109]*Engineering Record* (New York: McGraw Publishing Company, Ltd.) 67, no. 24 (June 14, 1913): p. 658.

[110]*Albertan*, February 28, 1913.

[111]*Ibid.*

[112]*Herald*, May 4, 1912.

[113]*Engineering Record* 67, no. 24 (June 14, 1913): p. 658.

[114]*Albertan*, February 28, 1912.

[115]*Engineering Record* 67, no. 24 (June 14, 1913): p. 658.

[116]*Albertan*, February 28, 1912.

[117]*Engineering Record* 67, no. 24 (June 14, 1913): p. 658.

[118]*Albertan*, February 28, 1912.

[119]*Ibid.; Engineering Record* 67, no. 24 (June 14, 1913): p. 658.

[120]*Albertan*, February 28, 1913.

[121]*Ibid.; Strathmore Standard*, April 8, 1912. GAI, Newspaper Clippings File.

[122]*Ibid.*

[123]*Albertan*, January 13, 1913.

[124]*Ibid.*

[125]*Albertan*, January 14, 1913.

[126]*Herald*, November 15, 1913.

[127]*Herald*, August 2, 1913.

[128]*Herald*, October 11, 1913.

[129]*Herald*, November 15, 1913.

[130]*Ibid.*

[131]*Herald*, July 19, 1912.

[132]*Herald*, June 26, 1909.

[133]Mumford, *Roots*, p. 22.

[134]GAI, Photo Archives.

[135]*Labour Gazette*, April, December 1910, June, 1911; *Albertan*, March 17, 1910; January 4, 1912.

# Conclusion

Between 1905 and 1914, Calgary's architectural landscape was drastically altered. The more than ten thousand buildings erected during this explosive decade demonstrate that the city arose not in isolation, but in conjunction with the rapid settlement of the western agricultural frontier. Wholesale houses, retail outlets, administrative offices, financial establishments, hotels, industries and a host of related enterprises quickly sprang up as opportunities for investment and profit flourished. Furthermore, sudden increases in the local population necessitated the construction of thousands of dwellings, in addition to the institutions and community services deemed essential for the well-being of residents. Changed economic and demographic circumstances thus created a need for more substantial architecture in Calgary. With the sudden surge in construction activity between 1909 and 1913, that need was met. Moreover, the identity of the community was speedily transformed. Where log structures had earlier stood as tell-tale reminders of the city's youthfulness, towering skyscrapers built of steel, concrete, brick and terra cotta now loomed over the horizon. Numerous schools and public buildings constructed with native sandstone added to the atmosphere of progress and achievement in the city, as did the impressive residences of the local élite. Meanwhile, the proliferation of workers' suburbs indicated that Calgary had also become an important source of labour, thus enhancing its potential as an industrial centre. In short, Calgary rapidly took on both the appearance and character of a major city. By 1914, it possessed many of the same attributes as much older cities to the east and south— economic affluence, an advanced physical environment and attendant urban sprawl. This study therefore supports J.M.S. Careless's interpretation of western Canadian urbanization, which argues that the urban west was virtually contemporaneous with the urban east by 1914 because of the rapid transference of metropolitan technology, capital, institutions and ideas.[1] By the time that World War I began, Calgary was thus a vigorous and ascendant urban centre, complete with all the physical characteristics—including buildings—of a modern, mature metropolis.

A close examination of the buildings erected between 1905 and 1914 has also revealed a number of salient details concerning Calgary architecture and society. First, Calgary's buildings were, in general, progressively larger, more expensive and more up-to-date with respect to design, structure and internal services. They were built increasingly with machine-made components, including reinforced concrete, structural steel, pre-cut and pre-assembled lumber and ceramic items. They also required less artful craftsmanship, and represented a more efficient use of manpower and materials. Such building trends were due essentially to the heightened demand for more numerous facilities of grander dimensions, escalating land and construction costs and the availability of industrially produced building materials during the boom years. Equally, they were influenced by the influx into the city of numerous architects, engineers and contractors who were familiar with the latest developments in building fashions and construction methods.

Second, it is apparent that certain building styles were more prevalent than others. The preference of impressive Edwardian classical forms for many of the sandstone schools, provincial government buildings and some commercial structures, Classical and Vernacular Revival motifs for the homes of the wealthy and Gothic imagery for churches suggests that among Calgary architects and patrons there was a distinct predisposition towards British architectural fashions. Many of Calgary's most active architects—W.S. Bates, F.J. Lawson, W.D. Major and Alex Pirie—were, in fact, British-trained.[2] Others, including G.M. Lang, W.S. Branton, Leo Dowler and J.J. O'Gara, came from central Canadian cities where they also gained exposure to British design ideas then in vogue.[3] Among members of the general public and the local élite, there was also a notable fascination with picturesque design ideas from Great Britain. The initial enthusiasm shown for Thomas Mawson's eccentric proposal to remake Calgary into a visionary Edwardian metropolis provides evidence of this esthetic inclination.[4]

Although British-inspired designs found favour in Calgary, it is also true that architectural forms currently popular in the United States were utilized. The Romanesque Revival style, exemplified in City Hall and earlier commercial buildings; the Beaux-Arts tradition, which found expression in the Boston-designed Carnegie Library; and the California Bungalow style, adopted in a large number of houses throughout the city, all illustrate the wide acceptance of fashions devised in the United States. The most obvious example of their impact on the local architectural landscape was the erection of tall commercial buildings, whose structural design, if not external styling, was derived from the Chicago School of modern architecture. But at the same time, it is significant that many of these American ideas were brought to Calgary via more mature Canadian cities including Montréal, Toronto, Winnipeg and Vancouver, where the exchange of building conventions was long established, and where buoyant economic conditions allowed for more diverse cultural expressions in local architecture.[5]

Third, an evaluation of building trends and stylistic preferences has provided much insight into the cultural milieu in Calgary during the pre-war era. On the one hand, Calgary buildings bore a remarkable resemblance to many structures in American cities, as did those in other major Canadian centres at the turn of the century. Common economic and social conditions induced by rapid urbanization, together with the increased circulation of new building designs and technology, led to the adoption of similar architectural solutions across North America. For this reason, many of Calgary's skyscrapers, industrial facilities and modern apartments could easily have been built in Chicago and St. Louis, or in Montréal and Winnipeg.

On the other hand, Calgary buildings were clearly manifestations of a predominantly British design influence. Tudor, Gothic and Edwardian Free Classical forms, while also popular in the United States during this period of strong Anglo-American relations, were associated with long-established British architectural traditions. Their extensive usage in Calgary by many British and Canadian architects suggests that local buildings had an important cultural purpose, particularly since the majority of residents were of Anglo-Celtic descent and generally looked to their homeland for cultural inspiration. In addition to imparting a certain dignity to the city, these designs represented British cultural images that were transplanted to a remote urban frontier. They served to remind the local citizenry of their origins and predestined fellowship in the British family of nations. They were thus emblematic of the fundamentally British character of society in Calgary, indeed in western Canada, before the war.

This book has also suggested that Calgary's architectural landscape was marked by obvious socio-economic class distinction. Calgary was, by 1914, not unlike other much older and larger cities in central Canada, or even in Great Britain, in this respect. The often flamboyant residences of the wealthy, set amidst park-like grounds in appealing subdivisions and in close proximity to numerous beautiful institutional buildings were a world apart from the multitude of working-class suburbs with their crowded bungalows, cottages, apartments and much humbler churches and schools. Even the work places of the city evidenced this growing spatial and emotional separation. Palatial office buildings, retail stores and banks in the downtown district lacked nothing in modern comfort and convenience and were far removed from the smoke and noise of Calgary's many industrial complexes located mainly in the southeast sector of the city.

Yet while these contrasts were apparent, they were to a great extent overshadowed by the boom. This was a decade of boundless optimism for all, both rich and poor. Opportunities for profit, business growth, employment and even social mobility were never as great in the city as before the war. It was an epoch of unfaltering faith in material progress, of unquestioning trust in continued prosperity and of unchallengeable confidence in Calgary's position as a dominant metropolis. The buildings erected between 1905 and 1914 were not only an index of the general wealth of the age, but also embodiments of this incredible hope. Only the realities of sudden economic depression and war were able to reveal that such optimism was largely unfounded.

# Notes

[1]J.M.S. Careless, "Aspects of Urban Life in the West, 1870-1914," in *Prairie Perspectives 2: Selected Papers of the Western Canadian Studies Conference, 1970 and 1971*, ed. A.W. Rasporich and H.C. Klassen, (Toronto: Holt, Rinehart and Winston, 1973), pp. 39-40.

[2]See W.S. Bates Papers; A.O. Jennings, *Calgary, Sunny Alberta the Industrial Prodigy of the Great West: Her Phenomenal Progress, Thriving Industry and Wonderful Resources* (Calgary: Jennings Publishing Company); and A.O. MacRae, *History of the Province of Alberta*, vol. 2, pp. 1015, 1016.

[3]See A.O. MacRae, *History of the Province of Alberta*, vol. 2, pp. 929, 930, 958, 959, 1021, 1022.

[4]Thomas H. Mawson, *The City of Calgary Past Present and Future* (Calgary: Thomas H. Mawson and Sons and the City of Calgary Planning Commission, 1914).

[5]See Alan Gowans, *Building Canada: An Architectural History of Canadian Life* (Toronto: Oxford University Press, 1966), pp. 51-53, 66-71, 101-103, 105-113.

# Select Bibliography

Abbreviations

GAI—Glenbow-Alberta Institute Library and Archives
PAA—Provincial Archives of Alberta

## I. Primary Sources

A. Government Documents and Publications

1. Federal Government

*Censuses of Canada*, 1901, 1911, 1921.

*Census of Population and Agriculture of the North-West Provinces*, 1906.

Holdsworth, D.W. and Mills, E.G. "The B.C. Mills Prefabricated System: The Emergence of Ready-Made Buildings in Western Canada." Canadian Historical Sites Occasional Papers in Archaeology and History, no. 14. Ottawa: Parks Canada, National Historic Parks and Sites Branch, 1975.

Kendal, Elaine. *The Development of Edmonton and Its Buildings.* Manuscript Report no. 257. Ottawa: Parks Canada, National Historic Parks and Sites Branch, 1977.

*Labour Gazette*, 1909-1914.

*Labour Gazette Supplement, Wages and Hours of Labour in Canada, 1901-1902.* Ottawa: Department of Labour, March 1921.

Mills, Edward. *The Early Court Houses of Alberta.* Manuscript Report no. 310. Ottawa: Parks Canada, National Historic Parks and Sites Branch, 1977.

Rostecki, R.R. *The Early Court Houses of Saskatchewan.* Manuscript Report no. 306. Ottawa: Parks Canada, National Historic Parks and Sites Branch, 1977.

## 2. Provincial Government

Alberta Culture, Historic Sites Service. Files on Potential Historic Sites. Edmonton: Old St. Stephen's College.

*Annual Reports of the Department of Education of the Province of Alberta*, 1906-1914. Edmonton: Government Printer, 1907-1915.

*Annual Reports of the Department of Public Works of the Province of Alberta*, 1906-1914. Edmonton: Government Printer, 1907-1915.

Lehr, John C. *Ukrainian Vernacular Architecture in Alberta*. Alberta Culture Occasional Papers Series no. 1. Edmonton: Alberta Culture, Historical Resources Division, Historic Sites Service, 1976.

Rasmussen, Mark. "The Alberta Inventory of Potential Historic Sites Program Explanation." Unpublished document, Alberta Culture, Historical Resources Division. Edmonton: October 1978.

_____. *The Inventory Field Training Manual*. Unpublished reference manual, Alberta Culture, Historical Resources Division. Edmonton: March 1979.

## 3. Municipal Governments

*Annual Reports of the City of Calgary*, 1907-1915. Calgary: City Clerk, 1908-1916.

*City of Calgary Municipal Manual*, 1913-1916. Calgary: City Clerk, 1913-1916.

City of Calgary Planning Department. "Potential Heritage Sites Evaluation." 4 vols. Unpublished report prepared by Crothers Pearson Consulting, 1976.

City of Victoria Heritage Advisory Committee. *Heritage Conservation Report*. Victoria: City of Victoria, 1975.

## B. Manuscripts, Collected Papers and Archival Materials

Alberta Association of Architects Collection. PAA.

Calgary Power Papers. GAI.

Calgary Public School Board Records and Plans. Department of Community Relations and Department of Architectural Services, Calgary Public School Board.

Canadian Pacific Railway Papers. GAI.

City Clerk's Papers. GAI.

City of Calgary Papers. GAI.

City of Calgary By-Laws. GAI.

Crown Lumber Plans and Business Papers. GAI.

Dr. D.M. Black Collection. GAI.

Fire Department Papers. GAI.

James Abel Hornby Papers. GAI.

James Richards Papers. GAI.

John Gillespie, Diary of a Stonemason, 1893-1915. GAI.

Newspaper Clippings File. GAI.

Original Blueprints of City Hall. GAI.

Private Correspondence between the General Manager and the Calgary Branch Manager of the Bank of Nova Scotia, 1912 and 1913. Bank of Nova Scotia Archives, Toronto, Ontario.

S. Koch, Collector. GAI.

Stevenson Raines Historical Material. Canadian Architectural Archives, The University of Calgary.

Thomas Underwood Papers. GAI.

Ursenbach, Charles. "Interview with W.A. Branton." February and March 1974. GAI.


C. Directories, Journals and Newspapers

*The Calgary Daily Herald*, 1905-1914.

*The Calgary News Telegram*, 1905-1914.

*Construction*. Vols. 1, 3-7. Toronto: n. pub., October 1907 — December 1915.

*Engineering Record.* Vols. 67-68. New York: McGraw Publishing Company, Ltd., January 1913 - December 1913.

*Henderson's Alberta Directory,* 1906, 1907, 1908, 1914.

*Henderson's Calgary Directory,* 1910-1915, 1922.

*The Morning Albertan,* 1905-1914.

*Tregillus-Thompson Greater Calgary Directory,* 1913.

D. Contemporary Books, Pamphlets and Catalogues

*Annual Reports of the Canadian Western Natural Gas, Light, Heat and Power Company,* 1912-1915. n.p.: n.pub., 1912-1915.

*Architecture: Some Beautiful Effects Obtained by Architects and Master Painters.* Montreal: Sherwin Williams Paints, 1914.

Bensusan, S.L., ed., *Calgary.* London: Hodder and Stoughton, 1912.

Blue, John. *Alberta Past and Present.* 3 vols. Chicago: Pioneer Historical Publishing Company, 1924.

*The British Columbia Mills, Timber and Trading Company Catalogue of Patented and Ready-Made Houses.* Vancouver: n.pub., 1905.

*Calgary Alberta 1906.* Calgary: Dawson Publishers, 1906.

*Calgary and Sunny Alberta Illustrated: The Official Souvenir of the Dominion Exhibition, 1908.* n.p.: n.pub., 1908.

Calgary and the Calgary Board of Trade. *Calgary, Alberta, the Land of Plenty.* Calgary: n.pub., 1907.

*Calgary Board of Trade Annual Report,* 1913. Calgary: n.pub., 1913.

Calgary Board of Trade. *First Annual Buyers' Guide.* Calgary: n.pub., 1913.

_____. *The Famous Calgary District.* Calgary: n.pub., 1906.

The Calgary Daily Herald. *Why Go to Canada?* Calgary: Herald Publishing Company, June 1910.

*Calgary, the City Phenomenal, the Continent's Fastest Growing City.* Winnipeg: Canadian Promotion Company, 1912.

Cockburn, James A. *Calgary, Alberta, the City of the Foothills in the Land of the Chinook, with its Commercial Houses, Churches, Residences, etc.— Portrayed.* n.p.: n.pub., 1905.

*The Engineering Works and Natural Resources of the City of Calgary and the Bow River Valley of Alberta.* Calgary: City of Calgary and the Engineers of Alberta, October 1915.

*Facts of Interest—Past and Present: First Baptist Church, Calgary, Alberta.* Calgary: n.pub., 1911.

Goad, Charles E. *Insurance Plan of Calgary, Alberta.* n.p.: Charles E. Goad, Civil Engineers, 1911 and 1913.

Jennings, A.O. *et al. Calgary, Sunny Alberta, the Industrial Prodigy of the Great West: Her Phenomenal Progress, Thriving Industry and Wonderful Resources.* Calgary: Jennings Publishing Company, 1911.

Linton Brothers Stationery. *The City of Calgary: The Commercial Capital of Sunny Alberta.* Calgary: Linton Brothers Stationery, 1911.

MacRae, A.O. *History of the Province of Alberta.* 2 vols. Calgary: The Western Canada History Company, 1912.

Mawson, Thomas H. *The City of Calgary Past, Present and Future.* Calgary: Thomas H. Mawson and Sons and the City of Calgary Planning Commission, 1914.

Morgan, Henry James. *The Canadian Men and Women of the Time.* Toronto: William Briggs, 1912.

*The 100,000 Manufacturing, Building and Wholesale Book Edition of the Morning Albertan.* Calgary: The Morning Albertan, 1914.

Parker, C.W., ed. *Who's Who in Western Canada.* Vancouver: Canadian Press Association, 1911.

_____. *Who's Who and Why.* Toronto: Canadian Press Association, vol. 2, 1912; and International Press

Ltd., vol. 3, 1913, vol. 6, 1915, vol. 7, 1916.

*Picturesque Calgary*. Calgary: Calgary Herald Publishing Company, 1900 and 1905.

*The Radford Architectural Company Stores and Flats Catalogue*. Chicago: n.pub., 1909.

Richardson, E.L. *Calgary, Alberta, the Commercial Metropolis of Western Canada*. Calgary: Hammond Lithographing, 1907.

Ruse, Joseph. *The Story of Calgary and Tuxedo Park*. Calgary: Land and General Investment Company, 1911.

*Souvenir of the Sixth Annual Assembly of the Royal Architectural Institute of Canada*. Calgary: M.J. Connoly, Publisher, 1913.

Souvenir of the Twenty-Seventh Annual Convention of the Trades and Labour Congress. n.p.: n.pub., 1911.

Thwaite, Leo. *Alberta: An Account of its Wealth and Progress*. London: George Routledge and Sons Ltd., 1912.

White, B.S. *The Story of Calgary—Alberta—Canada, Progress—Resources—Opportunities*. Calgary: Western Standard Publishing Company, 1914.

Wilson, L.C. *Souvenir of Calgary and District*. Calgary: n. pub., 1910.

# II. Secondary Sources

## A. Books and Booklets

Ames, Sir Herbert. *The City Below the Hill: A Sociological Study of a Portion of the City of Montreal*. Toronto: University of Toronto Press, 1972.

Andrews, Wayne, *Architecture, Ambition and Americans: A Social History of American Architecture*. New York: The Free Press, 1964.

Arthur, Eric. *Toronto: No Mean City*. Toronto: University of Toronto Press, 1964.

Ausubel, Herman. *The Late Victorians: A Short History.* Toronto: Van Nostrand Company Ltd., 1955.

Barrett, A.A. and Liscombe, R.W. *Francis Rattenbury and British Columbia: Architecture and Challenge in the Imperial Age.* Vancouver: University of British Columbia Press, 1983.

Barry, W.W. *An Anecdotal History of the Calgary Separate School Board.* Calgary: Calgary Separate School Board, 1967.

Beyer, Glenn H. *Housing and Society.* New York: The Macmillan Company, 1965.

Bland, J., and Mayrand, P. *Three Centuries of Architecture in Canada.* Montréal: Federal Publications Service, 1971.

Bond, C.C.J. *City on the Ottawa.* Ottawa: Queen's Printer for the Department of Public Works, 1965.

Brunskill, R.W. *Illustrated Handbook of Vernacular Architecture.* London: Faber and Faber, 1971; reprint ed., 1978.

Buckley, Kenneth. *Capital Formation in Canada, 1896-1930.* Canadian Studies in Economics, vol. 2. Toronto: University of Toronto Press, 1955; reprint ed., The Carleton Library Series, No. 77, Toronto: McClelland and Stewart Ltd., 1974.

Burchard, J., and Bush-Brown, A. *The Architecture of America: A Social and Cultural History.* Boston: Little, Brown and Company, 1961.

Byers, M.; Kennedy, J.; and McBurney, M. *Rural Roots: Pre-Confederation Buildings in the York District of Ontario.* Toronto: University of Toronto Press, 1976.

Carter, David. *Calgary's Anglican Cathedral.* Calgary: The Cathedral Church of the Redeemer, 1973.

*Communities of Calgary: From Scattered Towns to a Major City.* Calgary: Century Calgary Publications, 1975.

Condit, Carl. W. *American Building.* Chicago: University of Chicago Press, 1968.

Chapman, S.D., ed. *The History of Working-Class Housing: A Symposium.* Totowa: Rowman and Littlefield, 1971.

Current, W.R., and Current, K. *Greene and Greene: Architects in the Residential Style.* Fort Worth: Amon Carter Museum of Western Art, 1974.

d'Iberville-Moreau, Luc. *Lost Montreal.* Toronto: Oxford University Press, 1975.

Ferns, S.J., and Ferns, H.S. *Eighty-Five Years in Canada.* Winnipeg: Queenston House, 1979.

Fitch, J.M. *American Building: The Historical Forces that Shaped It.* Boston and Cambridge: Houghton Mifflin Company and the Riverside Press, 1947; reprint ed., 1966.

Fleming, J.; H. Honour, H.; and Pevsner, N. *The Penguin Dictionary of Architecture.* Harmondsworth: Penguin Books Ltd., 1943; reprint ed., 1975.

Foran, Max L. *Calgary An Illustrated History*, The History of Canadian Cities Series. Toronto: James Lorimer and Company and the National Museum of Man, 1978.

Fowke, Vernon C. *The National Policy and the Wheat Economy.* Toronto: University of Toronto Press, 1955; reprint ed., 1978.

Gilbert, Edward J. *Up the Years with the Saskatchewan Association of Architects*, n.p.: The Saskatchewan Association of Architects, 1970.

Girouard, Mark. *Life in the English Country House: A Social and Architectural History.* New Haven and London: Yale University Press, 1978.

*A Glossary of House Building Terms.* Ottawa: Central Mortgage and Housing Corporation, n.d.

Gowans, Alan, *Building Canada: An Architectural History of Canadian Life.* Toronto: Oxford University Press, 1966.

Greenhill, R. *The Face of Toronto.* Toronto: Oxford University Press, 1964.

Heritage Ottawa. *An Inventory of Architectural Records.* Ottawa: Minister of Supply and Services, Canada, and

Public Archives, Canada, 1978.

Hitchcock, H.R. *The Architecture of H.H. Richardson and His Times.* Hamden: Archon Books, 1966.

Hockman, J.; Kuziw, I.; Moir. G.; and Thorkelsson, I. *Early Buildings of Manitoba.* Winnipeg: Peguis Publishers, 1973.

Hubbard, R.H. *The Development of Canadian Art.* Ottawa: The National Gallery, 1963.

Inverness Field Club. *Old Inverness in Pictures.* Edinburgh: Paul Harris, Publishing, 1978.

Jordan, Robert Furneaux. *A Concise History of Western Architecture.* Norwich: Thames and Hudson, 1969; reprint ed., 1975.

_____. *Victorian Architecture.* Norwich: Jarrold and Sons Ltd. and Penguin Books, 1966.

Kalman, Harold. *The Railway Hotels and the Development of the Chateau Style in Canada.* Victoria: University of Victoria and the Maltwood Museum, 1968.

_____. *Explore Vancouver.* Vancouver: University of British Columbia Press, 1974.

Kirker, H. *California's Architectural Frontier,* n.p.: The Henry E. Huntington Library and Art Gallery, 1960; reprint ed., New York: Russel and Russel, 1970.

Kirkland, Edward C. *Dream and Thought in the Business Community, 1860-1890.* Ithaca: Cornell University Press, 1956.

Leonoff, Cyril E. *The Architecture of Jewish Settlements in the Prairies.* Winnipeg: Jewish Historical Society of Western Canada, 1975.

MacEwan, Grant. *Calgary Cavalcade: From Fort to Fortune.* Edmonton: Institute of Applied Art, 1958.

MacGregor, James G. *A History of Alberta.* Edmonton: Hurtig Publishers, 1972.

MacInnes, C.M. *In the Shadow of the Rockies*. London: Rivingtons, 1930.

MacRae, D.G.W. *The Arts and Crafts of Canada*. Toronto: Macmillan Company, 1944.

McNeill, Leishman. *Tales of the Old Town*. Calgary: Calgary Herald, 1951.

Mika, Nick. *Trenton, Past and Present*. Belleville: Mika Silk Screening, 1967.

Morrow, Joyce. *Calgary Many Years Hence*. Calgary: City of Calgary and The University of Calgary, 1978.

Mumford, Lewis. *Roots of Contemporary American Architecture*. New York: Reinhold Publishing Corporation, 1952; reprint ed., Dover Publications, 1972.

Norman Mackenzie Art Gallery. *Early Buildings of Saskatchewan*. Regina: University of Saskatchewan, 1967.

Pevsner, Nicholas. *An Outline of European Architecture*. Harmondsworth: Penguin Books Ltd., 1943; reprint ed., 1975.

Ritchie, Thomas. *Canada Builds, 1867-1967*. Toronto: University of Toronto Press and The National Research Council, 1967.

The Royal Architectural Institute of Canada. *Historic Architecture of Canada*. Ottawa: The Royal Architectural Institute of Canada, 1966.

Rubinstein, David. *Victorian Homes*. Newton Abbot: David and Charles Ltd., 1974.

Segger, Martin. *Victoria: A Primer for Regional History in Architecture*. Victoria: Heritage Architectural Guides, 1979.

Soby, Trudy. *A Walk Through Old Calgary*. Calgary: Century Calgary Publications, 1974.

_____. *Be It Ever So Humble*. Calgary: Century Calgary Publications, 1975.

Stamp, Robert M. *School Days, A Century of Memories*. Calgary: McClelland and Stewart West, 1975.

Stickley, Gustav. *Craftsman Homes—Architecture and Furnishings of the American Arts and Crafts Movement.* New York: Dover Publications, 1979; repr. Craftsman Publishing Company, 1909.

*The Story of Calgary.* Calgary: The 75th Anniversary Edition of the *Herald,* 1950.

Thompson, John H. *The Harvests of War: The Prairie West, 1914-1918.* Toronto: McClelland and Stewart, 1978.

Van Tighem, J.V. *History of the Calgary Separate School Board Researched From Old Records.* Calgary n.p., n.d.

Ward, Tom. *Cowtown, An Album of Early Calgary.* Calgary: McClelland and Stewart and the City of Calgary Electric System, 1975.

Williams, Vicky. *Calgary Then and Now.* Vancouver: Bodima Books Ltd., 1978.


B. Articles

Artibise, A.F.J. "Winnipeg and the City Planning Movement, 1910-1915." In *Western Perspectives 1: Papers of the Western Canadian Studies Conference, 1973,* edited by D.J. Bercuson, pp. 10-20. Toronto: Holt, Rinehart and Winston, 1974.

_____. "An Urban Economy: Patterns of Economic Change in Winnipeg, 1878-1971. *Prairie Forum* 1, no. 2 (November 1976): 166-185.

Brown, J. "Calgary, the City of the Foothills." *The Beaver* 11, no. 7 (April 1922): 2-4.

Buggey, Susan. "Researching Canadian Buildings: Some Historical Sources." *Social History* 10, no. 20 (November 1977): 409-426.

"The Buildings of Canada." *Explore Canada.* n.p.: *Readers' Digest* for the Canadian Automobile Association, 1974, pp. 409-421.

Careless, J.M.S. "Aspects of Urban Life in the West, 1870-1914." In *Prairie Perspectives 2: Selected Papers of the Western Canadian Studies Conference, 1970 and*

*1971*, edited by A.W. Rasporich and H.C. Klassen, pp. 25-40. Toronto: Holt, Rinehart and Winston, 1973.

Foran, Max L. "Urban Calgary, 1884-1895." *Social History* 5, no. 9 (April 1972): 61-76.

_____. "Land Speculation and Urban Development in Calgary, 1884-1912." In *Frontier Calgary: Town, City and Region, 1875-1914*, edited by A.W. Rasporich and H.C. Klassen, pp. 203-220. Calgary: McClelland and Stewart West, 1975.

Gowans, Alan. "The Canadian National Style." In *The Shield of Achilles: Aspects of Canada in the Victorian Age*, edited by W.L. Morton, pp. 208-219. Toronto: McClelland and Stewart, 1968.

_____. "The Evolution of Architectural Styles in Toronto." In *The Canadian City: Essays in Urban History*, Carleton Library Series, no. 109, edited by A.F.J. Artibise and G.A. Stelter, pp. 212-222. Toronto: McClelland and Stewart, 1977.

Holdsworth, D.W. "House and Home in Vancouver: Images of West Coast Urbanism, 1886-1929." In *The Canadian City: Essays in Urban History*, Carleton Library Series, no. 109, edited by A.F.J. Artibise and G.A. Stelter, pp. 186-211. Toronto: McClelland and Stewart, 1977.

Huel, Raymond C. "The Public School as Guardian of Anglo-Saxon Traditions: The Saskatchewan Experience, 1913-18." In *Ethnic Canadians: Culture and Education*, edited by Martin L. Kovacs, pp. 295-302. Regina: Canadian Plains Research Center, 1978.

Kalman, Harold. "Recent Literature on the History of Canadian Architecture." *Society of Architectural Historians Journal* 31 (December 1972): 315-323.

Katz, Michael B. "Class, Bureaucracy and Schools." *The Canadian Forum* (October-November 1972): 14-19.

Klassen, Henry C. "Life in Frontier Calgary." In *Western Canada Past and Present*, edited by A.W. Rasporich, pp. 42-58. Calgary: McClelland and Stewart West, 1975.

_____. "The 'Bond of Brotherhood' and Calgary Workingmen." In *Frontier Calgary: Town, City and Region, 1875-1914*, edited by A.W. Rasporich and Henry Klassen, pp. 267-271. McClelland and Stewart West, 1975.

Lehr, John C. "Ukrainian Houses in Alberta." *Alberta Historical Review* 21 (Autumn 1973): 9-15.

_____. "Changing Ukrainian House Styles." *Alberta History* 23 (Winter 1975): 25-29.

Lupton, A.A. "Cattle Ranching in Alberta, 1874-1910: Its Evolution and Migration." *Alberta Geographer* 3 (1966-67): 55-58.

Mathers, A.S. "Thirty-Five Years of Practice." *Journal of the Royal Architectural Institute of Canada* 32, no. 12 (December 1955): 462-464.

McDonald, Neil G. "Canadian Nationalism and North-West Schools, 1884-1905." In *Canadian Schools and Canadian Identity*, edited by Alf Chaiton and Neil McDonald, pp. 59-87. Toronto: Gage Educational Publishing, Ltd., 1977.

_____. "David J. Goggin: Promoter of National Schools." In *Shaping the Schools of the Canadian West*, edited by David Jones, Nancy Sheehan, and Robert Stamp, pp. 14-28. Calgary: Detselig Enterprises, 1979.

McGinnis, Janice P. Dickin. "Birth to Boom to Bust: Buildings in Calgary, 1875 - 1914." In *Frontier Calgary: Town, City and Region, 1875-1914*, edited by A.W. Rasporich and Henry Klassen, pp. 6-19. Calgary: McClelland and Stewart West, 1975.

Roe, F.G. "The Old Log House in Western Canada." *Alberta Historical Review* 6 (Spring 1958): 1-9.

_____. "The Sod House." *Alberta Historical Review* 18 (Summer 1970): 1-7.

Schlichtmann, Hansgeorg. "The 'Ethnic Architecture in the Prairies' Conference: A Report and a Geographer's Reflections." *Prairie Forum* 1, no. 1 (April 1976): 69-75.

_____. "Social Troubles in Calgary in the Mid-1890's." *Urban History Review*, No. 3-74 (February 1975): 8-16.

Smith, P.J. "Calgary, A Study in Urban Pattern." *Economic Geography* 38 (October 1962): 315-329.

_____. "Change in a Youthful City: The Case of Calgary, Alberta." *Geography* 56 (January 1971): 1-14.

Stamp, Robert M. "The Response to Urban Growth: The Bureaucratization of Public Education in Calgary, 1884-1914. In *Frontier Calgary: Town, City and Region 1875-1914*, edited by A.W. Rasporich and Henry Klassen, pp. 153-168. Calgary: McClelland and Stewart West, 1975.

_____. "Empire Day in the Schools of Ontario: The Training of Young Imperialists." In *Canadian Schools and Canadian Identity*, edited by Alf Chaiton and Neil McDonald, pp. 100-115. Toronto: Gage Educational Publishing, Ltd., 1977.

Thomas, Lewis G. "The Rancher and the City: Calgary and the Cattleman, 1883-1914." *Transactions of the Royal Society of Canada* 6, Series 4, Section 2 (June 1968): 203-215.

_____. "Alberta Perspectives, 1905." *Alberta History* 28 (Winter 1980): 1-5.

Van Nus, Walter, "The Fate of City Beautiful Thought in Canada, 1893-1930." *Historical Papers* (1975), pp. 191-210.

Voisey, Paul. "In Search of Wealth and Status: An Economic and Social Study of Entrepreneurs in Early Calgary." In *Frontier Calgary: Town, City and Region, 1875-1914*, edited by A.W. Rasporich and Henry Klassen, pp. 221-241. Calgary: McClelland and Stewart West, 1975.

# III. Unpublished Theses, Dissertations, Papers and Other Sources

Bourdon, David. "The Empire and the Alberta School System, 1905-1914." Seminar Paper, Department of History, University of Calgary, April 1980.

Breen, David H. "The Cattle Compact: The Ranch Community of Southern Alberta, 1881-1896." M.A. thesis, University of Calgary, 1969.

Bussard, L.H. "Early History of Calgary." M.A. thesis, University of Alberta, 1935.

Daniels, Leroi A. "The History of Education in Calgary." M.Ed. thesis, University of Washington, 1954.

Evans, Simon. "The Passing of a Frontier: Ranching in the Canadian West, 1886-1912." Ph.D. dissertation, University of Calgary, 1976.

Fedori, Marianne. "The History of Eau Claire: Changes in a Residential Community." Seminar Paper, Department of History, University of Calgary, April 1978.

——————. "Ethnic Residential Patterns: The Case of Bridgeland in Calgary." Seminar Paper, Department of History, University of Calgary, April 1979.

Foran, Max L. "The Calgary Town Council, 1884-1895: A Study of Local Government in a Frontier Environment." M.A. thesis, University of Calgary, 1975.

Gowans, Alan. "The Architecture of the First and Second British Empires." Public Lecture, Glenbow-Alberta Institute, March 27, 1979.

Holdsworth, D.W. "Vernacular Forms in an Urban Context: A Preliminary Investigation of Facade Elements in Vancouver Housing." M.A. thesis, University of British Columbia, 1971.

Macleod, H.L. "Properties, Investors and Taxes: A Study of Calgary Real Estate Investment, Municipal Finances, and Property Tax Arrears, 1911-1919." M.A. thesis, University of Calgary, 1977.

Macleod, Norman L. "The Calgary College, 1912-1915: A Study of an Attempt to Establish a Privately Financed University in Alberta." Ph.D. dissertation, University of Calgary, 1970.

McDonald, Neil G. "The School as an Agent of Nationalism in the Northwest Territories, 1884-1905." M.Ed. thesis, University of Alberta, 1971.

Rasmussen, Mark. Alberta Culture, Edmonton, Alberta. Interview, July 24, 1980.

Render, Lorne, "Calgary Architecture, 1884-1915." Manuscript for a slide show. Winter 1968. GAI.

Soby, Trudy. "Architectural Trends in Calgary's Downtown Core." Paper, December 1974. GAI.

Sproule, A.F. "The Role of Patrick Burns in the Development of Western Canada." M.A. thesis, University of Alberta, 1962.

Taraska, E.A. "The Calgary Craft Union Movement, 1900-1920." M.A. thesis, University of Calgary, 1975.

Utas, Gregory P. "Calgary Architecture, 1875-1915." M.E.Des. degree project, University of Calgary, 1975.

Wade, C.J. "Red River Architecture, 1812-1870." M.A. thesis, University of British Columbia, 1967.

Weston, Phyllis E. "The History of Education in Calgary." M.A. thesis, University of Alberta, 1951.

# Appendix A

## Selected Apartments: Residents and Their Occupations

Devenish Apartments (908 - 17th Avenue West)

Source: *Henderson's Calgary Directory*, 1912

| W.J. Duffy | bookkeeper, Crown Lumber |
| W.G. Soltan | clerk, Bank of Montreal |
| C.S.S. Watson | inspector of agent, Life Department, Royal Insurance Company |
| Douglas | (not available) |
| James McHaig | (not available) |
| O.G. Devenish | real estate and financial agent |
| Alwyn I. Danks | physician |
| H.W. Robinson | manager, Alberta Empress Company |
| A. Colyns | (not available) |
| John Miller | city clerk |
| Mrs. Agnes Dick | widow |
| R.G. Davies | electrical engineer |
| James Hart | superintendent, Tie and Timber Branch, C.P.R. |
| Geneva Stickney | stenographer, E.C. Metzner and Company |
| Grace Davies | (not available) |
| Clara Canty | (not available) |
| Miss E.J. Beattie | Elite Millinery Company |
| R.H. Kyle | (not available) |
| E.C. Stewart | secretary, Alberta Club |
| J.W. Glenwright | provincial manager, Prudential Life Insurance Company |

**Connaught Apartments** (710 - 4th Avenue West)

Source: *Henderson's Calgary Directory*, 1913

| J.B. Aylward | clerk, Calgary Paint and Glass Company |
| C.W. Roenish | secretary-treasurer, Western Co-op Grain Company |
| T.D. Spurrell | agent |
| G.M. Matthey | law student |
| W.M. Wyllie | real estate |
| Albert Prince | janitor |
| Edward Harrison | engineer |
| Charles G. Palmer | broker |
| Frank Rose | jeweller |

| Jean Duncan | stenographer |
| G.M. Ponton | mining engineer |
| J.F. McCarney | proprietor, Riverside Hotel |
| J.J. McLuckie | department manager |
| T.E. LeClaire | physician |
| L.M. Cochrane | manager, Northern Electric and Manufacturing |
| John M. Storey | manager, Seamen Kent Company, Limited |

**Morasch Block** (642 - 1st Avenue Northeast)

Source: *Tregillus-Thompson Greater Calgary Directory*, 1913

| Hendrich Schrieder | labourer |
| Peter Morasch | proprietor |
| Joseph Langlois | electrician |
| Joseph W. Marshall | motorman, City Street railway |
| Henry Morrall | labourer, Fyshe, McNeil, Martin, Trainer Company |
| Stephen Siegmeth | tinsmith |
| Herman Hein | barber |
| Adam Ghittie | (not available) |
| William McGregor | messenger |
| Alex Butler | steamfitter |
| William Berger | mechanic |
| Alex Weiss | (not available) |

**Sevenoaks Court** (1339 - 10th Avenue East)

Source: *Tregillus-Thompson Greater Calgary Directory*, 1913

| Peter Hoffman | engineer, C.P.R. |
| Ole Olson | fireman |
| Albert A. Prout | Prout McCall and Company |
| William H. Plant | foreman, C.P.R. |
| Byron Gagegas | fitter |
| Thomas Metcalfe | janitor |
| William Roberts | (not available) |
| Clarence A. Trimble | Prout McCall and Company |
| George G. Crabbe | travelling salesman |
| William F. Quebec | engineer, C.P.R. |

| William G. Dean | manager, east end branch, James Findlay Drug Co. |
| Harry B. Hennessy | driver |
| Wesley T. Doull | foreman, stickerman, Cushing Brothers Limited |
| Frank N. Peterson | engineer, C.P.R. |
| A.A. Guy | (not available) |
| Archibald Burnap | fireman, C.P.R. |
| Archibald [sic] | brakeman, C.P.R. |
| David S. Short | conductor, C.P.R. |
| Robert C. Carroll | physician |
| W.S. Carson | yardmaster, C.P.R. |
| C. Roy Pickett | brakeman, C.P.R. |
| Joseph Clement | switchman, C.P.R. |
| David S. Jenkins | fireman, C.P.R. |
| Jane McKitrick | widow |
| J. Garfield McKitrick | conductor, C.P.R. |

# Appendix B

## Selected Office Buildings and Their Occupants

**Grain Exchange Building** (813 - 1st Street West)

Source: *Henderson's Calgary Directory*, 1912.

Grain Exchange Pool Room
Shoe-shine Stand
T.C. Choutris
Columbia Valley Irrigated Fruit Land, Limited
Alberta Home Builders, Limited
Western Agencies and Development Company
Beiseker and Davidson
Scott and Hartronft Real Estate
J.K. Lee and Company Real Estate
Ontario Fire Insurance Company
J.E. Rice and Company Real Estate
Western Canada Fire Insurance Company
Alix Loan and Investment Company

Johnstone and Ordas, Men's Furnishings
Alberta Pacific Elevator Company, Limited
Globe Elevator Company, Limited
Thomas M. Greig, Tailor
Dominion Grain Inspector's Office
W. Carson and Company, Grain Dealers
West Coast Grain Company, Limited
Royal Grain Company, Limited
Alberta Grain Company, Limited
Calgary Grain Exchange, Limited
CPR Telegraphs
Baird and Botterell, Grain Brokers
International Realty
James Richardson and Sons, Limited, Grain Merchants
E.M. Wallbridge, Grain Merchants
Wallbridge Elevator Company, Limited
North-West Grain Company, Limited
Cummings Grain Company, Limited
Standard Agencies, Limited, Real Estate
R.O. Benell, Contractor
Northern Grain Company, Limited
American Consulate
Vancouver Milling and Grain Company, Limited
National Elevator Company, Limited
Bertrand de Chaiance, Financial Agent
Alberta British Columbia Insurance Agency, Limited
Callingham and Company
Callingham Brown and Compny
Hardy and McFarlane
Ernest L. Martin, Plumber
New York Life Insurance Company
Leighton and Gilbert, Farm Lands
Clay and Maxwell, Dentists
Webb, Read, Hegan, Callingham and Company
J.A. McPhee Insurance Agency
Robb Engineering Company
K.S. Smith
Hodgson, Bates and Beattie, Architects

**Herald Building** (622 - 1st Street West)

Source: *Henderson's Calgary Directory*, 1914.

D.E. Black and Company, Jewellers
Herald Publishing Company, Limited
Herald Editorial Department
Canadian Newspaper, Limited
M.B. O'Farrell and Company, Brokers
Alberta Black and Silver Fox Company, Limited
Ten Twenty One Oil Company of Alberta, Limited
M.W. Macdonald, Barrister
Harcourt O'Reilly
E.V. Robertson, Barrister
London Scottish-Canadian Investment Syndicate, Limited
Alex Robertson
Kilbourn-Newton, Limited
Calgary and Sweetgrass Oil Fields, Limited
E.P. Howard
A.J. Danks, Physician
Hornibrook, Whittemore and Allan, Insurance
London Life
Lathwell and Waters, Barristers
W.J. Budd and Company, Limited, Real Estate
Keystone Portland Cement Company, Limited
Keystone Oil Company, Limited
Alert Oils, Limited
Beaver Oils, Limited
Cameron and Anderson, Real Estate
Chinook Oil Company, Limited
Minerva Oils, Limited
E. Campbell Pugh, Broker
Perpetual Rights Oil Company, Limited
Crown Brokerage Company
Western Pacific Oil Company, Limited
North West Pacific Oil Company, Limited
M.M. Pease, Coursetier [sic]
C.T. and W.H. McGuffin, Physicians
D.R. Dunlop, Physician
H.W. De Renzy, Dentist
A.B. Singleton, Physician
Bungalow Construction Company
F.E. Eaton, Barrister

Building Superintendent Office
A.C. Moss, Chiropody
Victor Oil Company, Limited
Morrissey Oil and Coal, Limited
Amalgamated Oil Company, Limited
W.D. Gow, Barrister
Central Detective Service of Canada
H.W. McGill, Physician
J.I. Kelly, Dentist
H.B. and J.H. Millican, Dentists
Caledonia Oil Company, Limited
Tulsa Oil and Gas Company, Limited
Sun Life Assurance Company of Canada
R.G. Barnes and Company, Brokers
Eagle Oil Company, Limited
M. Mecklenburg, Optician
Taber Transit Company
British Columbia Life Assurance Company
Standard Investment Company
A.E. Finch and Company, Investments
Black Rock Oil Company, Limited
Calgary Add Club
C.E. Hicks
Edmund Limited, Loans
London Glasgow Oil Company, Limited
Calgary Electrotyping Company, Limited
T.M. Fyshe, General Contractor
North West Drilling Company, Limited
British Alberta Oil Company, Limited
Craig Cunningham
Berkeley Mowbraw, Limited
Unity Oils, Limited
Athabasca Oils, Limited
Crawford and Russell, Brokers
Adanac Brokerage Company
North West Empire Land Company, Limited
Goodison and Ross, Financial Brokers
R.W. Mayhew and Company, Real Estate
Bruce, Peare and Robinson, Financial Agents
Lone Star Oil and Gas Company, Limited
H.L. Fridenberg
Marwick Mitchell, Peat and Company

Melbourne Brokerage Company, Limited
Midway Drilling Company, Limited
Britannia Oil and Natural Gas Company, Limited
H.E. Halsell, Wholesale Labour
Wendling-Nathan Labour Company, Limited
National Supply Company, Limited
McParland and Company, Limited, Brokers
McTavish Brothers, Brokers
Western Canadian Oil Company, Limited
Hutcharm Limited, Advertising Agents
T.V. Orr, Advertising Counselor
Langner and Company, Brokers
Lion Oil Company, Limited
Peerless Oil Works, Limited
Pittsburg Oil Company, Limited
Grease Creek Oil Company, Limited
Circle Synod Number One, Limited
Record Oil Company, Limited
Granby Oil Company, Limited
Harlan and Company, Stock Brokers
W.S. Scott, Barrister
Alliance Investment Company of Canada, Limited
A.W. Pryce-Jones, Broker
Western Canada Accounting and Guarantee Insurance
Company
W.B. Blair, Insurance Agent
Sterling Coal Company, Limited
E.E. Taylor, Real Estate
Western Natural Resources
Western Coal Operators Association
E.A. Ray, Public Stenographer
H.R. Johnson, Geologist
Calgary Stock Exchange
J.H. Pope, Broker
G.A. Touche and Company, Accountants
T.M. Fysche, General Contractor
Western Securities Corporation, Limited
Alberta Petroleum, Limited

**Lougheed Building** (604 - 1st Street West)

Source: *Henderson's Calgary Directory*, 1914

P.W. McCrystle, Tailor
Matinee Company, Limited
Bowness Estates, Limited
J.J. Mason, Insurance Agent
Butters and McCallum, Real Estate
Abraham Kadish, Cigars
Grand Theatre
Fred Harling, Tailor
A.M. Terrill, Limited, Florist
Carmichael Drug Company, Limited
Dominion Gresham Guarantee and Casualty Company
Scott Black Sales Company
Gresham Life Assurance Society, Limited
H.G. Riblet, Civil Engineer
Hook Construction Company
Stone and Clay, Limited
G.A. Crozier, Tailor
P.J. Lydiatt
Sherman Theatre Offices
Mountain Pine Agencies Limited
Turnbull and Crichton, Manufacturers' Agents
Ulster Linen Company
R.H.L. O'Callaghan
Lougheed Building Office
Imperial Coal Company
M. and E. Lumber Company, Limited
Canada Touring Company, Limited
N.R. Weber, Real Estate
Birnie Lumber Company, Limited
A. Ritchie, Contractor
E. MacDonell, Chiropody
Daykin and Jackson, Limited
International Supply Company, Limited
Southern Cross Oil Company, Limited
W.C. Daniel and Company, Brokers
C.N. Railway Freight Office
Western Life Assurance Company
Bow Island Gas and Calgary Oil Company, Limited
Summit Engineering Company, Limited

Brett and Kelly Real Estate
W.E. Jull
Vitrified Clays, Limited
Hudson, Oscar, and Company, Accountants
Tuec Company of Alberta, Limited
Rotary Club of Calgary
Alberta Farmers Co-operative Elevator Company, Limited
Interstate Land Company
C.E. Lasher, Real Estate
H.L. Niles, Real Estate
Empress Realty Company, Limited
Grain Growers Grain Company, Limited
N.J. Dinnen and Company, Limited, Machinist
F.B. Fisenden, Public Stenographer
Lettermay Oil and Delivery Company, Limited
Multigraph Sales Company, Limited
Southern Alberta Oil Company, Limited
G. Grossman, Engineer
Ponthiere Charnace, Real Estate
Turner Valley Oil Company, Limited
Bond Adams Company
P. Lyall and Sons, Limited
Sutherland Realty, Limited
Fruit Dispatch Company
Moose Mountain Oil Company, Limited
Ranchmen's Gas and Oil Company, Limited
Brown and Vallance, Architects
Western Canada Properties, Limited
Mecca Oil and Gas Company, Limited
C. Nunnemaker, Insurance Agent
Voss Brothers, Contractors
Sinclair and Allen, Geologists
Mason and Hickey, Commercial Merchants
E.H. McGuire and Company, Brokers
J.O. Beattie, Real Estate
Hewitt and Luke, Brokers
Pioneer Oil Company, Limited
Stoner, Lockwood and Wheeler, Limited, Well Drillers
C.E. Coffey
Metropolitan Life Insurance Company
Agencies Limited, Insurance
R.S. Thomas, Hair-dresser
Western Canada Fire Underwriters' Association

G.E. Rodwell, Insurance Agent
A.H. Brigham
United Farmers of Alberta
Calgary Petroleum Products Company, Limited
Shaws Domestic Bungalows
Moxam Realty and Construction Company, Limited
Henderson Grant, Manufacturers' Agents
Tregillus Clay Products Company
Canadian New Towns, Limited
Harrison, White and Barker, Importers
Canadian Consolidated Engineering Company
F.C. Watson
H.A. Setheringham
F.A. Walker
W. Nesbitt
W. Wallance
G.M. Fowler
A.W. Mackinnon
J.T. Todd
O.O. Davies
A. Veitch
A.E. Logan
H. Cronn
H.E. Burbidge
G.S. Whitaker
M.E. White
Mark Drum
William Little
P.L. Naismith
F.M. Compton
C.B. Morris
D.B. Forbes
H.N. White
B.F. Croan
G.W. Bowers
University Club Rooms
James M. Baker
Judge A.A. Carpenter
Dr. Paul Faber
Bertrand de Charnace
P.J. Bergeron
H. de Ponthiere

J.G. Edgar
Herbert W. Whitehead
T.A. McAuley

**Canada Life Building** (303 - 8th Avenue West)

Source: *Henderson's Calgary Directory* , 1914

Northern Trusts Company
Canadian Fire Insurance Company of Winnipeg
Northern Mortgage Company of Canada
Canadian Indemnity Company
U.S. Fidelity and Guarantee Company
Equitable Life Assurance Society of the United States
Imperial Guarantee and Accidental Insurance Company
 of America
Robin Hood Milling Company
Commonwealth Trust Company, Limited
F.L. Hazard, Physician
G.R. Johnson, Physician
Dominion of Canada Guarantee and Accidental Insurance
 Company
Western Cordage Company
Newton and Nowers, Financial Agents
Alberta Land Company, Limited
Ocean Accidental and Guarantee Corporation
Post Office Inspector
Williams and West, Accountants
Regent Oil Company, Limited
Christian Science Reading Room
Inland Revenue Department
Post Office Railway Mail Service
Clarke, McCarthy, Carson and MacLeod, Barristers

This book is one of a series published jointly by Alberta Culture and the Canadian Plains Research Center. Their common objective is to bring to public notice the diverse aspects of Alberta history as evidenced in Alberta's historical resources. Each is a result of scholarly research by a specialist who has approached the significant historical topic from the vantage point of the associated historic sites.

# Index

198

## C

## G

## H

# N

Natural Gas, 69
Nielson Block, 130
North America, eastern tenements, 68
    eclectic landscape of, 116
    urban growth in, 66
North Calgary School, 98
*News Telegram*, 34, 35
Nunn, Mr., 55

# O

Ogden CPR Repair Shops, 20, 23, 33, 61, 151-152, 153
Ogden, I.E., 151
O'Gara, J.J., 72, 165
Olivet Baptist Church, 113
Oriental influences on architecture, 56
Osborne, F.E., 31
Otis Fenson Elevators, 145

# P

Packham, George, 55
Palliser Hotel, 32, 131, 143, 146, 147
Panama Canal, 34, 35, 132
Parks Canada. *See* Canadian Inventory of Historic Buildings
Park Hill School, 98
Pearce, William, 49
Phyllis Apartments, 74
*Pièce-sur-pièce* log construction, 11
Pioneer Tractor Company, 23, 34
Pirie, Alex, 71, 165
Poffenroth Apartments, 74
Portage La Prairie, 34
Post Office, 31, 35
Price, Alfred, 55
    residence of, 54, 55
Prince, Peter, 49
Prudential Builders Limited, 64
    "Calgary Model," 64
Pryce-Jones Company department store, 33, 131
Public Buildings, 89, 103-117,
    Carnegie Library. *See* Public Library
    City Hall, 32, 88, 103-107
    Court House, 32, 88, 107-109, 123n
    Fire Department Headquarters, 32
    Fire Hall Number One, 109, 110
    Grain Exchange Building, 32, 51, 131-134
    Land Titles Office, 88, 106, 108
    Post Office, 31, 35

## U

Ukrainian folk buildings, 11
Underwood, Thomas, 49
Underwood Block, 32, 86n
United States, 66, 67, 112, 128
    architectural styles of, 165-166
    aesthetic and technological trends in, 30
    construction techniques in, v
University of Calgary, 112
Utas, George, 13

## V

Vacancy rates, 58
Vancouver, 11, 12, 147, 166
Vendome Block, 74
Vernacular Revival Movement. *See* Domestic Revival Style
Victoria, 10, 49
    Heritage Advisory Committee, 10
    Heritage Conservation Report, 10
Victoria Block, 51
Vivian, Henry, 75

## W

Wade, Jill, 11
Walker, Col. James, 48, 84n
Warehouses
    Ashdown, 31, 130
    Blow, 130
    Ellis and Grogan, 32
    International Harvester, 32, 130
    McDougall and Forster, 33, 131
    Tees and Persse, 31, 130
Westbourne Baptist Church, 113
Western Canada
    architectural history of, 1, 8
    history, 1
    architecture, 9
Western Block, 86n
Western Milling Company, 53
Westinghouse, Church, Kerr and Company, Consulting and
  Constructing Engineers of New York and Montreal, 152
West Mount Pleasant School, 98
Winnipeg, 49, 91, 112, 129, 131, 141, 147, 148
Working class housing, 23, 47, 57-69
    issue of, 59-61
    shortage of, 57
    in Vancouver, 11-12

# Y

DATE DU